American ENGLISH FILE

Workbook

Christina Latham-Koenig
Clive Oxenden
Paul Seligson

Paul Seligson and Clive Oxenden are the original co-authors of
English File 1 and *English File 2*

OXFORD
UNIVERSITY PRESS

Contents

STUDY LINK iChecker SELF-ASSESSMENT CD-ROM

Powerful listening and interactive assessment CD-ROM

Your iChecker disc on the inside back cover of this Workbook includes:

- **AUDIO** – Download ALL of the audio files for the Listening and Pronunciation activities in this Workbook for on-the-go listening practice.

- **FILE TESTS** – Check your progress by taking a self-assessment test after you complete each File.

Audio: When you see this symbol iChecker, go to the iChecker disc in the back of this Workbook. Load the disc in your computer.

1

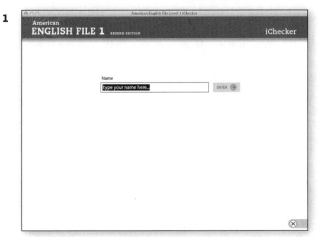

Type your name and press "ENTER."

2

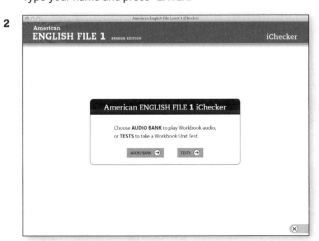

Choose "AUDIO BANK."

3

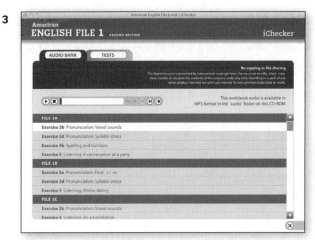

Click on the exercise for the File. Then use the media player to listen.

You can transfer the audio to a mobile device from the "audio" folder on the disc.

File test: At the end of every File, there is a test. To do the test, load the iChecker and select "Tests." Select the test for the File you have just finished.

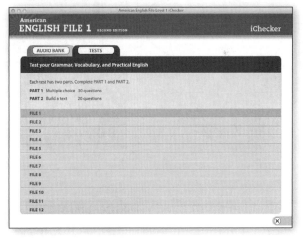

1A My name's Hannah, not Anna

1 GRAMMAR verb *be* ⊞, subject pronouns

a Complete column 1 with the words in the box. Then write the contractions in column 2.

| she | are | they | is | + | are | is | are |

1 Full form	2 Contraction
I am	1 *I'm*
you 2 _____	3 _____
he 4 _____	5 _____
6 _____ is	7 _____
it 8 _____	9 _____
we 10 _____	11 _____
you 12 _____	13 _____
14 _____ are	15 _____

b Complete the sentences with *be*. Use a contraction.

1 *I'm* four.

2 _____ students.

3 _____ in room 2.

4 _____ Thursday.

5 _____ in a taxi.

6 _____ tourists.

7 _____ in room 317.

8 Hello. _____ in my class.

2 VOCABULARY days of the week, numbers 0–20, greetings

a Put the letters in order to make days of the week. Remember to start with a CAPITAL LETTER.

1 ARSAYDUT   *Saturday*

2 NYAUDS   _____

3 HRDYTUSA   _____

4 ODNYMA   _____

5 DFARYI   _____

6 DSYEEAWND   _____

7 EUASDTY   _____

b Continue the series.

1 five, six, seven, *eight*, *nine*, *ten*.

2 six, eight, ten, _____, _____, _____.

3 twenty, nineteen, _____, _____, _____.

4 five, seven, nine, _____, _____, _____.

c Complete the dialogues.

1 **A** Hi, Emily. ___This___ is Daniel.
  B Hello, Daniel. _____ to _____ you.

2 **A** Hi, I'm Paulo. _____ 's your _____?
  B Louise.
  A _____?
  B Louise!

3 **A** Hi, Yoshi. _____ are you?
  B I'm fine, thanks. And _____?
  A Very well, thank you.

4 **A** What's your phone _____?
  B It's 718-555-0123.

d Complete the words with *a, e, i, o,* or *u.*

1 S_e_ _e_ y_o_ _u_.

2 S___ y___ _n Fr__d__y.

3 N__, n__t Fr__d__y. S__t__rd__y!

4 S__rry. S___ y___ __n S__t__rd__y.

5 By__.

6 G___dby__.

3 PRONUNCIATION vowel sounds, word stress

a Write the words in the chart.

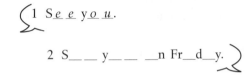

fish	tree	cat	egg	train	bike

b **iChecker** Listen and check. Then listen again and repeat the words.

c <u>Underline</u> the stressed syllable in these words.

1 sand|wich
2 te|nnis
3 eigh|teen
4 thir|teen
5 bas|ket|ball
6 good|bye
7 e|mail
8 In|ter|net
9 com|pu|ter
10 ho|tel

d **iChecker** Listen and check. Then listen again and repeat the words.

4 LISTENING

iChecker Listen to three conversations. Choose a, b, or c.

1 Sarah's phone number is…
  a 917-555-6942.
  b 917-555-6542.
  c 917-555-6524.

2 The class on Thursday is in…
  a room two.
  b room three.
  c room five.

3 A cheese sandwich and a coffee cost…
  a five dollars and twenty cents.
  b four dollars and twenty cents.
  c five dollars and ten cents.

USEFUL WORDS AND PHRASES

Learn these words and phrases.

bye /baɪ/
fine /faɪn/
goodbye /gʊdˈbaɪ/
hello /həˈloʊ/
hi /haɪ/
sorry /ˈsɑri/
thank you /ˈθæŋk yu/
thanks /θæŋks/
very well /ˈvɛri wɛl/
How are you? /haʊ ɑr yu/
Nice to meet you. /ˈnaɪs tə ˈmit yu/

How can you govern a country
which has 246 varieties of cheese?

Charles de Gaulle, French politician

1B All over the world

1 GRAMMAR verb *be* ☐? and ☐−

a Complete B's sentences.

1 **A** Seoul is in China.
   B *It isn't in China, it's in* South Korea.

2 **A** Lady Gaga is British.
   B _____ American.

3 **A** He's Mexican.
   B _____ Peruvian.

4 **A** Istanbul and Ankara are in Greece.
   B _____ Turkey.

5 **A** We're in room 219.
   B _____ room 309.

6 **A** Parmesan is from France.
   B _____ Italy.

7 **A** You're Brazilian.
   B _____ Argentinian.

8 **A** Enrique Iglesias is American.
   B _____ Spanish.

b Order the words to make questions.

1 your / 's / name / What
   What's your name _____ ?

2 she / Where / 's / from
   _____ ?

3 America / from / they / South / Are
   _____ ?

4 five / room / we / in / Are
   _____ ?

5 vacation / you / Are / on
   _____ ?

6 from / he / Vietnam / Is
   _____ ?

c Match these answers to the questions in **b**.

a Yes, he is. ☐
b No, I'm not. ☐
c She's from Italy. ☐
d No, we aren't. ☐
e Yes, they are. ☐
f Michael. ☐ *1*

2 VOCABULARY the world, numbers 21–100

a Complete the sentences with a country or a nationality.

1 Luz is from Peru. She's *Peruvian*.
2 Bratwurst is German. It's from _*Germany*_ .
3 Aki is from Japan. He's _____.
4 My friends are Iranian. They're from _____.
5 Maria is from Mexico. She's _____.
6 Kia cars are South Korean. They're from
   _____.
7 Paella is from Spain. It's _____.
8 We're Thai. We're from _____.
9 She's from the United States. She's _____.
10 They're Brazilian. They're from _____.

b Complete the dialogues with a continent.

1 **A** Where's Spain?
   B It's in _____.

2 **A** Where's Japan?
   B It's in _____.

3 **A** Where's Brazil?
   B It's in _____.

4 **A** Where's Canada?
   B It's in _____.

c Complete the compass.

d Write the numbers
   in words.

1 27 _*twenty-seven*_
2 33 _____
3 40 _____
4 48 _____
5 56 _____
6 62 _____
7 74 _____
8 85 _____
9 99 _____
10 100 _____

3 PRONUNCIATION /ə/, /tʃ/, /ʃ/, /dʒ/

a (Circle) the syllable with /ə/ in these words.

1 A|fri|ca
2 Chi|na
3 Ger|ma|ny
4 Ire|land
5 Eur|ope
6 Bra|zil
7 I|ta|ly
8 Ja|pan

b **iChecker** Listen and check. Then listen again and repeat the words.

c (Circle) the word with a different sound.

tʃ chess	1	**Ch**inese Engli**sh** Fren**ch**
ʃ shower	2	Turki**sh** Ru**ss**ian Vietname**s**e
dʒ jazz	3	Spani**sh** **J**apanese Ar**g**entinian

d **iChecker** Listen and check. Then listen again and repeat the words.

4 READING

Read about three people: Yin, Moira, and Carlos. Mark the sentences T (true) or F (false).

1 Moira is a teacher.   _T_
2 Carlos is a student.   __
3 Moira is twenty-eight. __
4 Yin is a teacher.   __
5 Yin is from Asia.   __
6 Carlos is nineteen.   __
7 Yin is twenty-eight.   __
8 Moira is American.   __

5 LISTENING

iChecker Listen and complete the dialogues.

1 **A** Are you _____?
  B No, I'm Turkish. I'm from Istanbul.

2 **A** Where are you from?
  B We're _____. We're from
  _____. We're on vacation in South America.

3 **A** Where's he from? Is he _____?
  B No, he isn't. He's _____. He's from Cancún.

4 **A** Mmm, delicious. Is it _____?
  B No, it isn't. It's _____.

USEFUL WORDS AND PHRASES

Learn these words and phrases.

flag /flæg/
language /ˈlæŋgwɪdʒ/
Excuse me… /ɪkˈskyuz mi/
I'm from… /ˈaɪm frɑm/
All over the world. /ɔl ˈoʊvər ðə wərld/
I'm not sure. /aɪm nɑt ʃʊr/
Where are you from? /wɛr ɑr yu ˈfrɑm/

This is Yin. He's 19 and he's a student. Yin is Chinese. He's from Shanghai, a big city in the east of China.

This is Moira. She's an English teacher and she's 28. Moira is Canadian. She's from Vancouver, a city in the west of Canada.

This is Carlos. He's Mexican. He's from Monterrey, an important city in the North of Mexico. Carlos is 25 and he's a receptionist in a hotel.

1C Open your books, please

1 GRAMMAR possessive adjectives: *my, your*, etc.

a Complete the chart.

Subject pronouns	Possessive adjectives
I	1
2	your
he	3
4	her
5	its
we	6
you	7
8	their

b Complete the sentences with a possessive adjective.

1 _Her_ name's Teresa.
2 _____ name's Edward.
3 We're students. _____ teacher's name is Matt.
4 I'm Brazilian. _____ family is from São Paulo.
5 It's a Chinese restaurant. _____ name is Merry City.
6 **A** What's _____ phone number?
   B My cell phone number? It's 917-555-0156.
7 They're Canadian. _____ last name's Baker.

c Order the words to make questions.

1 first / her / What's / name
  A _What's her first name_?
  B Sandra.
2 teacher / Where / from / your / 's
  A _____?
  B The United States.
3 he / student / Is / a
  A _____?
  B No, he isn't.
4 you / old / How / are
  A _____?
  B I'm 35.
5 name / last / spell / do / How / you / your
  A _____?
  B C-O-O-M-B-S.

2 INSTRUCTIONS IN YOUR BOOK

Match the words to the pictures.

a complete [3]
b underline [ ]
c match [ ]
d circle [ ]
e ask your partner [ ]

f put an ✗ [ ]
g cover the text [ ]
h number [ ]
i check [ ]
j cross out [ ]

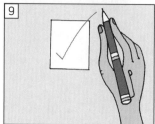
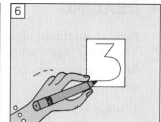
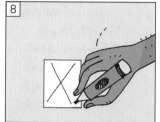

3 VOCABULARY classroom language

a Complete the sentences.

1 C_lose_ the door.
2 L_____ and repeat.
3 O_____ your books, please.
4 W_____ in pairs.
5 A_____ the question.
6 T_____ off your cell phone.
7 L_____ at the board.
8 G_____ to page 94.

b Order the words to make sentences.

1 don't / I / know
   I don't know. .

2 do / How / it / you / spell
   _____?

3 don't / I / understand
   _____.

4 you / that / can / please / repeat / Sorry,
   _____?

5 in / English / Excuse / what's / me, / "vacaciones"
   _____?

6 remember / I / can't
   _____.

4 PRONUNCIATION /oʊ/, /u/, /ɑr/; the alphabet

a Circle the word with a different vowel sound.

oʊ phone	know	don't	north
u boot	two	south	you
ɑr car	**Ar**gentinian	st**ar**t	vocabul**ar**y
oʊ phone	g**o**	cl**o**se	d**o**

b iChecker Listen and check. Then listen again and repeat the words.

c Circle the letter with a different vowel sound.

eɪ train	i tree	u boot	ɛ egg	aɪ bike
H J G	C P S	Q U O	F A M	E I Y

d iChecker Listen and check. Then listen again and repeat the letters.

5 LISTENING

iChecker Listen to the dialogue at a hotel reception desk. Complete the form.

First name	1 _Erik_
Last name	2 _____
Country	3 _____
City/State	4 _Miami, Florida_
Address	5 _Atkinson Road_
Zip code	6 _____
Email address	7 _____
Phone number	8 _305 -_
Cell phone number	9 _305 -_

USEFUL WORDS AND PHRASES

Learn these words and phrases.

address /əˈdrɛs/
age /eɪdʒ/
zip code /ˈzɪp koʊd/
receptionist /rɪˈsɛpʃənɪst/
student /ˈstudnt/
last name /ˈlæst neɪm/
first name /ˈfərst neɪm/
cell phone /ˈsɛl foʊn/
phone number /ˈfoʊn nʌmbər/
How old are you? /haʊ ˈoʊld ɑr yu/
I'm 22. /aɪm twɛnti ˈtu/

iChecker TESTS FILE 1

1 VOCABULARY In a hotel

Complete the words.

1 the e*levator*_____ 4 r_____
2 a s_____ room 5 the f_____ fl_____
3 a d_____ room

2 CHECKING IN

Complete the conversation with phrases in the box.

| Can you sign here, please? | ~~I have a reservation~~ |
| Just a second... | Thank you | That's right |

A Good evening, sir.
B Hello. [1] *I have a reservation*_____. My name's Carl Zimmerman.
A Can you spell that, please?
B Z-I-M-M-E-R-M-A-N.
A Thank you. For three nights?
B Yes. [2] _____.
A Can I have your passport, please?
B [3] _____ Here you are.
A Thank you. [4] _____ Thank you.
   Here's your key. It's room 403, on the fourth floor. The
   elevator is over there. Enjoy your stay, Mr. Zimmerman.
B [5] _____.

3 SOCIAL ENGLISH

Complete the missing words in the dialogue.

1 A Who is this?
   B Th*is*__ is David Barnsley.
2 A Where are you from?
   B I'm from Boston. What a_____ you?
3 A Sorry.
   B No pr_____.
4 A Hello?
   B Is th_____ Tom?
5 A Are you on vacation?
   B No. I'm here on b_____.
6 A Is 10:30 OK for you?
   B That's p_____.
7 A Would you like another drink?
   B No thanks. It's t_____ for bed.

4 READING

a Match the hotels to the people. Write the numbers
   in the boxes.

   1 Antonia and James want to have a relaxing weekend.
   2 Mr. Edwards wants to have a two-day meeting
      with managers from other US offices.
   3 The Scott family wants to go to Boston and visit
      the city.

Sheraton
One Audubon Road
Wakefield, MA 01880

280 double rooms
Conference center
Restaurant
Wi-fi connection
12 miles from Logan
International Airport

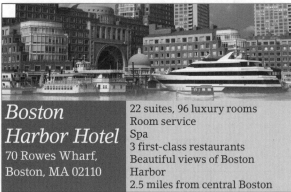

Boston Harbor Hotel
70 Rowes Wharf,
Boston, MA 02110

22 suites, 96 luxury rooms
Room service
Spa
3 first-class restaurants
Beautiful views of Boston
Harbor
2.5 miles from central Boston

Hotel Marlowe
25 Edwin H. Land
Boulevard
Cambridge, MA 02141

236 family-friendly rooms
Children stay for free
Wi-fi connection
Fitness center
Free morning coffee and tea
2.1 miles from the central Boston

b Underline five words or phrases you don't know.
   Use your dictionary to look up their meaning and
   pronunciation.

My favorite things in life
don't cost any money.
Steve Jobs, American founder of Apple

2A A writer's room

1 VOCABULARY things

Complete the crossword.

Clues across ➡

Clues down ⬇

2 W A L L E T

2 GRAMMAR a / an, plurals; *this / that / these / those*

a Write *It's + a / an* or *They're*.

1 _It's a_ change purse.
2 _They're_ pens.
3 _____ dictionary.
4 _____ umbrella.
5 _____ stamps.
6 _____ keys.
7 _____ ID card.
8 _____ pencil.

b Write each word in its plural form in the correct column.

pencil ~~city~~ ~~coin~~ ticket nationality watch window
address sandwich country class dictionary

-s	-es	-ies
coins	*addresses*	*cities*

c Complete the sentences with *this, that, these,* or *those.*

1 _That_'s a French newspaper.

2 _____ watch
is American.

3 _____ are my
headphones!

4 _____ book
is good.

5 _____ are
your keys.

11

d Complete the chart.

Singular	Plural
man	
	women
person	
	children

e Complete the sentences with a word from the chart in **d**.

1 Her mother is a very nice __*person*__ .
2 My English teacher is a _____ . His name's William.
3 I have two _____ . My first _____ is six years old.
4 Many American _____ drink coffee.
5 Not that restroom, Mr. Davis! It's for _____ , not _____ .

3 PRONUNCIATION final –*s* and –*es*; *th*

a (Circle) the word that ends in /ɪz/.

1 coins	wallets	(change purses)
2 classes	files	scissors
3 stamps	books	addresses
4 photos	watches	headphones
5 tissues	pens	sandwiches
6 magazines	glasses	newspapers

b **iChecker** Listen and check. Then listen again and repeat the words.

c (Circle) the word with a different sound.

mother ð	1 that	they	thanks
thumb θ	2 thing	thirty	these
mother ð	3 three	this	the
thumb θ	4 Thursday	those	thirteen

d **iChecker** Listen and check. Then listen again and repeat the words.

4 READING

Read the text and label the pictures.

The **top five** things in people's bags

Keys are at the top of the list. They can be house keys, car keys, or office keys. Next are pens, to write down names, numbers, and email addresses. Number three on the list is a package of tissues. These can be white or different colors, like pink or yellow. Next is medicine, for example aspirin for a bad head. Receipts are number five on the list. These are small pieces of paper from stores.

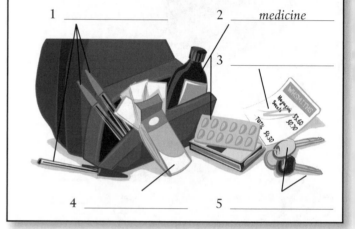

1 _____
2 __*medicine*__
3 _____
4 _____
5 _____

5 LISTENING

iChecker Listen to four people talking about things they have in their bags. Which person…?

1 has a book in his / her bag that helps him / her speak to people
2 has something to listen to music
3 changes bags every day
4 has a computer in his / her bag

USEFUL WORDS AND PHRASES

Learn these words and phrases.

lamp /læmp/
room /rum/
neat /nit/
messy /ˈmɛsi/
What's this in English? /wɑts ðɪs ɪn ˈɪŋglɪʃ/

2B Stars and Stripes

1 GRAMMAR adjectives

a (Circle) the correct words.

1 They're **jeans blue** / **blue jeans**.
2 It's a **nice day** / **day nice**.
3 My sisters are **very tall** / **very talls**.
4 That's a **car fast** / **fast car**.
5 These are **goods photos** / **good photos**.
6 Those boots are **really cheap** / **really cheaps**.
7 It's a **big house** / **house big**.
8 Her children aren't **very olds** / **very old**.

b Order the words to make sentences.

1 blue / This / is / a / pen
   *This is a blue pen*_____.

2 expensive / an / That's / watch
   _____.

3 very / My / long / hair / is
   _____.

4 rich / very / is / woman / That
   _____.

5 boots / really / Your / dirty / are
   _____.

6 city / This / a / dangerous / is
   _____.

7 very / book / good / That / isn't / a
   _____.

8 big / house / very / is / His
   _____.

2 VOCABULARY colors, adjectives, modifiers: *very / really*

a Write the colors.

1 blue + yellow = ___*green*___
2 black + white = _____
3 red + yellow = _____
4 white + red = _____
5 red + green = _____

b Complete the crossword. Write the opposite adjectives.

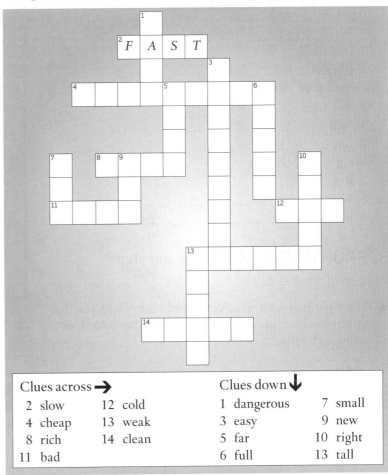

Clues across →

2 slow	12 cold	
4 cheap	13 weak	
8 rich	14 clean	
11 bad		

Clues down ↓

1 dangerous	7 small
3 easy	9 new
5 far	10 right
6 full	13 tall

c Match the pictures to the sentences. Write the letter in the box.

1 She's thin, with long hair. [B]
2 He's tall, with short hair. ☐
3 He's old, and good-looking. ☐
4 She's young, with blond hair. ☐
5 He's short, with dark hair. ☐
6 She's fat, and she's beautiful. ☐

d Look at the information and write sentences with *is very* (adjective) *isn't very* (adjective), or (adjective).

	Rob	Neil	Jim
Age	15	65	85
Height	6 feet, 5 inches	5 feet, 2 inches	5 feet, 9 inches
Weight	300 pounds	250 pounds	121 pounds

Age (old/young)

1 Rob *is very young/isn't very old.*
2 Neil *is old.*
3 Jim _____ .

Height (tall / short)

4 Rob _____ .
5 Neil _____ .
6 Jim _____ .

Weight (fat / thin)

7 Rob _____ .
8 Neil _____ .
9 Jim _____ .

3 PRONUNCIATION long and short vowel sounds

a Make phrases with an adjective and a noun with the same vowel sound. Write the phrases in the chart. Use *a* / *an* with singular nouns.

Adjectives
blue   clean   good   long   ~~big~~   stop
Nouns
book   ~~city~~   watch   jeans   shoes   song

fish	1 *a big city*	saw	4 _____
tree	2 _____	bull	5 _____
clock	3 _____	boot	6 _____

b 🔲 **iChecker** Listen and check. Then listen again and repeat the words.

4 READING

Read the text and write T (true) or F (false).

1 The Walk of Fame is in the UK.   —
2 It's a short street.   —
3 Every year there are more stars.   —
4 The stars are for famous actors.   —
5 Michael Jackson has more than one star.   —
6 Only real people can have a star.   —

THE HOLLYWOOD WALK OF FAME

Hollywood is an area of Los Angeles in California in the US. The Walk of Fame is in the center of the area on Hollywood Boulevard and Vine Street. It is over 1.2 miles long, and has more than 2,400 stars. There are more than 20 new stars every year.

The stars are in five different types: movies, TV, music, radio, and theater. Some famous people have more than one star, for example, Michael Jackson. He has two stars: one as a solo artist, and one as a member of the Jackson Five. But the Walk of Fame isn't only for real people. Mickey Mouse has a star and more recently, Shrek.

5 LISTENING

🔲 **iChecker** Listen to five speakers describing celebrities with Hollywood stars. Which speaker describes…?

A a short singer with blond or brown hair   —
B an old American actor with dark eyes   —
C a tall, good-looking man with brown eyes   —
D an actor and musician with blue eyes   —
E a British woman with green eyes   —

USEFUL WORDS AND PHRASES

Learn these words and phrases.

actor   /ˈæktər/
actress   /ˈæktrəs/
eyes   /aɪz/
hair   /hɛr/
musician   /myuˈzɪʃn/
politician   /ˌpɑləˈtɪʃn/
sportsman   /ˈspɔrtsmən/
sportswoman   /ˈspɔrts‚wʊmən/
singer   /ˈsɪŋər/
about (50)   /əˈbaʊt/
famous   /ˈfeɪməs/
What color is it?   /wɑt ˈkʌlər ɪz ɪt/

2C After 300 feet, turn left

1 GRAMMAR imperatives, *let's*

a Complete the sentences with a verb in the box.
Use a ⊞ or a ⊟ imperative.

be close come drink park slow speak turn worry

1 The city is dangerous at night. Please __*be*__ careful.
2 It's cold in here. Please _____ the window.
3 It isn't a problem. Please _____ about it.
4 This is an English class. Please _____ Spanish.
5 Their house is on this street. Please _____ down.
6 _____ on! We're late!
7 This is a bus stop. Please _____ here.
8 _____ that water – it's dirty.
9 This music is terrible. Please _____ it off.

b Match the sentences to the pictures.

A Let's park here.	D Let's cross the road here.
B Let's go home.	E Let's go to a hotel.
C Let's eat lunch there.	F Let's turn on the air conditioning.

2 VOCABULARY feelings

Write a sentence from the box.

I'm angry. I'm bored. I'm cold. I'm happy. I'm hot. I'm hungry. I'm sad. I'm stressed. I'm tired. I'm thirsty. I'm worried.

1 My friend is late. __*I'm angry.*__
2 It's 37° F. _____
3 It's my birthday! _____
4 My mother is in the hospital. _____
5 It's time for dinner. _____
6 I don't know what to do. _____
7 It's 100° F. _____
8 It's very late. _____
9 My husband is very far away. _____
10 I want water. _____
11 I have a lot of work. _____

3 PRONUNCIATION understanding connected speech

a Practice saying the sentences.

1 Look at those children.
2 Turn off the TV.
3 Let's ask that man.
4 Don't open the window.
5 Let's eat at home.
6 Sit on this chair.

b **iChecker** Listen and check. Then listen again and repeat the sentences.

c Complete the chart with the words in the box.

angry fat happy have hungry matter Monday one
sad ugly does young

🐱 cat	⬆ up
angry	

d 🔵iChecker Listen and check. Then listen again and repeat the words.

4 READING

a Read the article about tips for a long car trip. Match the headings to the paragraphs.

Have fun!   Is your car ready?   ~~Plan your trip.~~
Make sure everything is in the car.   Keep awake!

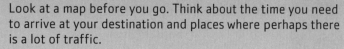

- **A**   _Plan your trip._
  Look at a map before you go. Think about the time you need to arrive at your destination and places where perhaps there is a lot of traffic.

- **B** _____
  Accidents sometimes happen because cars are in bad condition. Check the engine, the lights, and the wheels. Take the car to the garage if necessary.

- **C** _____
  Put your bags and everything you want to take with you in the hall the night before. Don't forget essential documents like passports or ID cards, and of course your driver's license.

- **D** _____
  Being tired is very dangerous for drivers. If you are tired, stop at a service station. Have a coffee or sleep for 15 minutes. In the car, open the windows and turn the radio on.

- **E** _____
  Children are often difficult during long trips. Take games, for example, computer games or word games, and iPods to listen to music. And don't forget things to eat and drink.

b Underline five words you don't know. Use your dictionary to look up their meaning and pronunciation.

5 LISTENING

🔵iChecker Listen to the dialogues and choose a, b, or c.

1 Where are they?
   a at an airport
   b at home
   c in a restaurant

2 Where are they?
   a in a hotel
   b in a car
   c in a restaurant

3 Where are they?
   a in a plane
   b in a hotel
   c in a car

4 Where are they?
   a in a restaurant
   b at home
   c in a car

5 Where are they?
   a in a hotel
   b at an airport
   c at home

USEFUL WORDS AND PHRASES

Learn these words and phrases.

jacket /ˈdʒækət/
pants /pænts/
sign /saɪn/
skirt /skərt/
uniform /ˈyunəˌfɔrm/
great (_opposite_ terrible) /greɪt/
left (_opposite_ right) /lɛft/
park (_verb_) /pɑrk/
stop /stɑp/
trip /trɪp/
with /wɪθ/
Be quiet! /bi ˈkwaɪət/
Don't worry. /ˈdoʊnt ˈwʌri/
Slow down. /sloʊ ˈdaʊn/
turn on (_opposite_ turn off) /ˈtərn ɑn/

🔵iChecker **TESTS** FILE 2

A perfect summer day is when the sun is shining, the breeze is blowing, the birds are singing, and the lawn mower is broken.

James F. Dent, American humorist and political cartoonist

3A Things I love about the US

1 VOCABULARY verb phrases

Complete the verb phrases.

animals	~~dinner~~	economics	homework	German
glasses	a new car	a newspaper	sorry	an umbrella

1 cook   _dinner_
2 study _____
3 speak _____
4 read _____
5 say _____
6 wear _____
7 do _____
8 like _____
9 want _____
10 take _____

2 GRAMMAR simple present ⊞ and ⊟

a Circle the correct words.

1 A lot of American people **has** / **have** pets.
2 It **don't rain** / **doesn't rain** a lot in my country.
3 You **live** / **lives** in a beautiful house.
4 The sun **shine** / **shines** a lot in Southern California.
5 My father **don't cook** / **doesn't cook**.
6 My brother **don't wear** / **doesn't wear** glasses.
7 Americans **don't eat** / **doesn't eat** fast food every day.
8 We **need** / **needs** a new computer.
9 My Canadian friend **make** / **makes** good coffee.
10 I **don't do** / **doesn't do** housework.

b Look at the chart and complete the sentences.

	Ryan	Kim
eat fast food	✓	✗
wear jeans	✗	✓
drink water	✓	✓
do housework	✓	✗
play the guitar	✗	✗

1 Ryan _eats_ fast food.
2 Ryan _____ jeans.
3 Ryan and Kim _____ water.
4 Kim _____ housework.
5 Ryan and Kim _____ the guitar.

6 Kim _____ fast food.
7 Kim _____ jeans.
8 Ryan _____ housework.

c Complete the sentences.

1 I _don't play_ (not play) tennis.
2 They _____ (not go) to the movies.
3 She _____ (have) two children.
4 Her father _____ (not work) in an office.
5 It _____ (rain) a lot.
6 We _____ (live) in a big apartment.
7 My friend _____ (not speak) English.
8 My friends _____ (study) at Tufts University.
9 You _____ (not do) your homework.

3 PRONUNCIATION vowel sounds, third person -s

a Say the words. Is the vowel sound the same or different? Write **S** (the same) or **D** (different).

1 say   take   ☐ S
2 do   go   ☐ D
3 drink   live   ☐
4 want   have   ☐
5 give   drive   ☐
6 call   walk   ☐
7 read   eat   ☐
8 feel   wear   ☐
9 play   watch   ☐
10 buy   like   ☐

b **iChecker** Listen and check. Then listen again and repeat the words.

c Circle the word which ends in /ɪz/.

1 likes   works   dances
2 lives   drinks   watches
3 drives   finishes   plays
4 uses   takes   speaks
5 studies   listens   kisses
6 changes   gives   wears

d **iChecker** Listen and check. Then listen again and repeat the words.

4 READING

a Read the text. Match the headings (A–D) to the paragraphs.

A Enjoy your dinner.
B Shopping on the street
C Traveling is so easy!
D We can find that for you.

Things I love about South Korea

Carly Hamilton is American, but she lives in Seoul, South Korea. Here are some things she loves about living there.

1 _____

In South Korea, the customer is really important. When you walk into a store, the salespeople greet you with a smile and say, "Hello." As you shop, they ask you if you need help. If you can't find something you want, the salespeople try to find it for you. They want you to be happy.

2 _____

I love restaurants that serve South Korean meat. It's so delicious. The servers grill the meat, and then they cut it for you! They also serve *banchan*—little side dishes of vegetables. The servers are very busy in South Korean restaurants. They don't talk as much as servers in the US, but they make sure that you have a great meal!

3 _____

There are so many places to shop in South Korea! People sell things like clothes and jewelry on the street. There are shopping booths in the subway stations, too! When I take the subway to work, I often buy a pretty bracelet or necklace because they're so cheap. It's really nice!

4 _____

The transportation system is great here! It's easy to get around because there are signs, and a lot of them are in English! You can use your cell phone on the subway here, too. You can't do that in the US!

b Guess the meaning of the highlighted words. Check in your dictionary.

5 LISTENING

iChecker Listen to the three speakers talking about Britain. Answer the questions with **H** (Hannah), **L** (Lina), or **J** (Julianna).

Hannah, Korea   Lina, Brazil   Julianna, the US

Who…?

1 doesn't like the food ☐
2 likes eating food from many different countries ☐
3 likes the atmosphere at work ☐
4 likes the parks ☐
5 thinks the traffic is terrible ☐
6 thinks that people are nice to foreigners ☐

USEFUL WORDS AND PHRASES

Learn these words and phrases.

love /lʌv/
rain /reɪn/
buy (*opposite* sell) /baɪ/
call /kɔl/
change /tʃeɪndʒ/
feel /fil/
need /nid/
pay /peɪ/
prefer /prɪˈfər/

I like to work: it fascinates me.
I can sit and look at it for hours.

Jerome K. Jerome, British writer

3B Work and play

1 VOCABULARY jobs

a Complete the crossword.

Clues across ➡   Clues down ⬇

b Complete the job descriptions with a verb from the list.

~~work~~ earn speak drive have work travel wear

1 "I ¹ __work__ inside and outside during the day or at night.
I ² _____ a car and sometimes I walk along the street.
I don't ³ _____ a lot of money. I ⁴ _____ a uniform."

2 "I work in an office with a computer, or outside with other people.
I ⁵ _____ French and Spanish and I sometimes
⁶ _____ to different countries. I don't wear a uniform.
I ⁷ _____ for a newspaper."

3 "I wear a uniform and I work with other people. I ⁸ _____ a
college degree, but I don't ⁹ _____ a lot of money.
I work during the day or at night, but I don't work outside.
I ¹⁰ _____ in a hospital."

c Match the descriptions to a job.

a journalist ☐   a nurse ☐   a police officer ☐

c Write -er or -or.

1 soccer play_er_   4 hairdress____
2 manag____   5 doct____
3 teach____   6 lawy____

d Complete the sentences with these words.

a an ~~at~~ for in retired unemployed

1 He studies economics __at__ school.
2 My brother is _____ engineer.
3 We work _____ an American company.
4 I don't have a job. I'm _____.
5 Paola is _____ receptionist.
6 My grandparents are 75. They're _____.
7 They work _____ a factory.

e Complete the words.

1 j*acket*   2 sh_____   3 t_____

4 sk_____   5 t_____   6 p_____

2 GRAMMAR simple present ☐

a Complete the questions with *Do* or *Does*.

1   *Do*   you work in an office?
2 _____ your parents speak foreign languages?
3 _____ your sister drive?
4 _____ you have a college degree?
5 _____ your mother work?
6 _____ James travel a lot?
7 _____ your father earn a lot of money?
8 _____ they wear a uniform?
9 _____ Ann walk to work?
10 _____ you work on the weekend?

b Complete the questions with *does*, *do*, *is*, or *are*. Then match the questions to the answers.

1 What   *does*   she do? ☐ c   a He's an actor.
2 What _____ they do? ☐   b In a restaurant – she's a waitress.
3 _____ he an architect? ☐   c ~~She's a doctor.~~
4 What _____ you do? ☐   d No, they're lawyers.
5 _____ they police officers? ☐   e I'm a hairstylist.
6 Where _____ she work? ☐   f No, he's an engineer.
7 _____ she a student? ☐   g They're pilots.
8 What _____ he do? ☐   h No, she's a teacher.

3 PRONUNCIATION /ər/

a Underline the stressed syllable.

1 ar|chi|tect   5 jour|na|list   9 re|cep|tion|ist
2 den|tist   6 mo|del   10 sol|dier
3 en|gi|neer   7 mu|si|cian
4 tea|cher   8 pi|lot

b **iChecker** Listen and check. Then listen again and repeat the words.

c (Circle) five more words with /ər/ and write them in the chart.

airport (earn) engineer Europe far here nurse journalist service short sure thirsty tired worker

ər bird	*earn* _____
	_____ _____
	_____ _____

d **iChecker** Listen and check. Then listen again and repeat the words.

4 LISTENING

a **iChecker** Listen to a contestant on a quiz show and (circle) his job.

administrative assistant dentist flight attendant
lawyer nurse receptionist veterinarian

b **iChecker** Complete the questions with the verbs in the box. Then listen again and check.

earn have ~~make~~ speak travel wear work

1   *Do you make*   things?
2 _____ a college degree?
3 _____ foreign languages?
4 _____ a uniform?
5 _____ for your work?
6 _____ a lot of money?
7 _____ with other people?

USEFUL WORDS AND PHRASES

Learn these words and phrases.

degree /dɪ'gri/
jacket /'dʒækət/
pants /pænts/
skirt /skərt/
comfortable /'kʌmftəbl/
foreign (languages) /'fɔrən/
earn money /ərn 'mʌni/
It depends. /ɪt dɪ'pɛndz/

It's relaxing to go out with my ex-wife
because she already knows I'm an idiot.

Warren Thomas, American writer

3C Meeting online

1 GRAMMAR word order in questions

a Order the words to make questions.

1 heavy / like / you / metal / Do
   Do you like heavy metal ?

2 the / do / on / do / What / weekend / you
   _____ ?

3 kind / What / do / books / read / you / of
   _____ ?

4 drink / want / another / you / Do
   _____ ?

5 a / Are / flight / you / attendant
   _____ ?

6 live / Where / do / Seattle / you / in
   _____ ?

7 is / favorite / Who / writer / your
   _____ ?

8 old / How / you / are
   _____ ?

9 iPad / have / you / an / Do
   _____ ?

10 your / good / Is / salad
   _____ ?

b Martin and Beth are new friends. They go for a coffee. Complete the questions.

M So, Beth, [1] _____where do you live_____ ?
B South of Denver. In a big apartment.
M [2] _____ _____ _____ with your parents?
B No, I live with my sister. [3] _____ _____ _____ any brothers and sisters?
M I have a sister. She's 23.
B [4] _____ _____ a student?
M No, she works. She's a salesperson.
B What about you? [5] _____ _____ _____ work?
M In a hotel.
B [6] _____ _____ _____ your job?
M Yes, I do. I love it!

2 VOCABULARY question words

Complete the questions with the questions words in the box.

How	How many	What	What kind	When
Where	Which	Who	Why	

1 A ___How___ do you go to work?
  B By car.
2 A _____ car do you drive?
  B A Toyota.
3 A _____ do you work?
  B In a factory.
4 A _____ do you go to the gym?
  B On Tuesdays and Thursdays.
5 A _____ do you prefer, the movies or the theater?
  B The theater, I think.
6 A _____ of music do you like?
  B Pop.
7 A _____ CDs do you have?
  B About a hundred.
8 A _____ is your favorite singer?
  B Rihanna.
9 A _____ do you like her?
  B Because she has a great voice.

3 PRONUNCIATION question words; sentence stress

a Match the question words 1–7 to the words with the same sounds a–g.

1 why	☐	a you
2 which	☐	b but
3 who	☐	c there
4 what	☐	d my
5 how	☐	e ten
6 when	☐	f rich
7 where	☐	g now

b **iChecker** Listen and check. Then listen again and repeat the words.

c <u>Underline</u> the stressed words.

1 **A** <u>What</u> do you <u>do</u>?
2 **B** I'm a doctor.
3 **A** Where do you work?
4 **B** I work in a hospital.

d **iChecker** Listen and check. Then listen again and repeat the sentences.

4 READING

a Read the article. Is *Facebook* good for your love life? _____

Love on *Facebook* f

Is *Facebook* good for your love life? Read on to find the answer.

1 C
You don't want to see your ex-boyfriend when your relationship finishes. And you really don't want to know about his new girlfriend. But *Facebook* tells you everything, including how happy he is with his new girlfriend.

2 ☐
Your boyfriend doesn't write on your "wall" one day. You're worried. Does it mean he doesn't like you? Another day, he sends you ten messages. You feel stressed. Does he like you too much?

3 ☐
Your friends know you have a new boyfriend because you change your status from "single" to "in a relationship." The problem is they know when it finishes too, because you change it back to "single" again.

4 ☐
You get a lot of messages from boys, but this isn't good for your relationship. When your boyfriend sees you writing to so many other boys, he feels worried. And that can mean the beginning of the end.

b Read the article again. Match the headings A–D to the paragraphs 1–4.

A No secrets on *Facebook*
B Popularity is dangerous
~~C Too much information~~
D What does he *really* feel?

5 LISTENING

a **iChecker** Max and Jessica meet in a restaurant for dinner. Listen to the conversation. Are they a good match? _____

b **iChecker** Listen again and mark the sentences T (true) or F (false).

1 Max and Jessica meet in a Japanese restaurant.   *T*
2 They have the same job.   __
3 They work for the same airline.   __
4 They like the same movies.   __
5 Jessica lives near the movie theater.   __
6 Max wants to go to the movies next Sunday.   __

USEFUL WORDS AND PHRASES

Learn these words and phrases.

movies /ˈmuviz/
TV shows /ˈtivi ʃouz/
Me too. /mi tu/
meet a partner /mit ə ˈpɑrtnər/
Really? /ˈrili/
Who's your favorite (actor)? /huz yər ˈfeɪvərət/
How interesting! /haʊ ˈɪntrəstɪŋ/
What about you? /wɑt ˈəbaʊt yu/

iChecker **TESTS** **FILE 3**

22

1 VOCABULARY Telling the time

Write the times.

1 *It's two*
thirty.   2 _____   3 _____   4 _____

5 _____   6 _____   7 _____   8 _____

2 BUYING A COFFEE

Order the dialogue.

1	A	Can I help you?
	B	No thanks. How much is that?
	A	Anything else?
	B	Thanks.
	A	$3.65. Thank you. And your change.
	B	Sorry, how much?
	A	Regular or large?
2	B	Yes. Can I have a latte, please?
	A	That's $3.65, please.
	B	To take away.
	A	To have here or to go?
	B	Large, please.

3 SOCIAL ENGLISH PHRASES

Complete the sentences with the words in the box.

a seat   first time   to drink   to you   ~~we are~~

1 Here __*we are*__ . This is the office.
2 Is this your _____ in Brazil?
3 Would you like something _____?
4 Talk _____ later.
5 Take _____ .

4 READING

a Read about some coffee shops in Seattle, Washington. In which shop can you…?

1 celebrate a friend's birthday
2 pay nothing to hear music
3 get your coffee very quickly
4 buy things for your house
5 learn about different kinds of coffee

A **BAUHAUS BOOKS AND COFFEE**   **301 East Pine Street**

This coffee shop serves some of the best coffee in Seattle. It also sells books and paintings—you can shop and drink coffee at the same time! Not interested in shopping? Sit at a table and use the wi-fi connection.

B **VICTROLA COFFEE AND ART**   **411 15th Avenue East**

A big coffee shop with a lot of space and beautiful art on the walls. There is free live music two or three times a week. The baristas are friendly and the coffee is great. So is the carrot cake.

C **TRABANT COFFEE AND CHAI**   **1309 Northeast 45th Street**

Trabant Coffee and Chai is open every day for breakfast, brunch, snacks, lunch, and dinner. All the food is homemade and vegan food is available, too. This coffee shop also gives classes about coffee.

D **C&P COFFEE COMPANY**   **5612 California Avenue Southwest**

A husband and wife run this coffee shop. It is in a beautiful, old house. It's a very calm and relaxing place, and the coffee is delicious. You can have a party or meeting in this coffee shop.

E **ZEITGEIST**   **171 South Jackson Street**

This coffee shop is popular because it serves great coffee. The friendly baristas can make drinks very fast. And they don't make mistakes. Zeitgeist is also a fun place to be with friends. There's a lot of space and many comfortable chairs.

b Guess the meaning of the highlighted food words. Check the meaning and pronunciation in your dictionary.

A celebrity is a person who works hard all his life to become well-known, then wears dark glasses to avoid being recognized.

Fred Allen, American comedian

1 VOCABULARY family

a Complete the chart.

¹ *grandmother*	grandfather
mother	²
³	uncle
wife	⁴
⁵	brother
daughter	⁶
⁷	nephew
cousin	⁸

b Complete the sentences.

1 My father's brother is my ___uncle___ .
2 My sister's daughter is my _____ .
3 My mother's sister is my _____ .
4 My father's mother is my _____ .
5 My aunt's daughter is my _____ .
6 My brother's son is my _____ .

2 GRAMMAR *Whose...?*, possessive *'s*

a Order the words to make sentences.

1 in / work / father's / my / store / I
  I work in my father's store .
2 Japanese / husband's / My / car / is
  _____ .
3 girlfriend's / is / His / Argentinian / mother
  _____ .
4 Sandra's / Do / know / you / brother
  _____ ?
5 live / wife's / with / parents / my / We
  _____ .
6 of / money / earns / friend / son's / a / Their / lot
  _____ .
7 dangerous / Is / job / Adam's
  _____ ?
8 uniform / very / Rosa's / ugly / is
  _____ .

b Add an apostrophe (') in the correct place in these sentences.

1 Carlos is my brother's friend.
2 That is my parents car.
3 I think this is that womans pen.
4 They drink coffee in the teachers room.
5 Do you know Barbaras sister?
6 My grandparents house is in Canada.
7 James wife is Brazilian.

c Look at the *'s* in these sentences. Write a letter in the box: **A** = possessive, **B** = *is*.

1 Kate's sister is a lawyer. [A] 5 Their uncle's a pilot. [ ]
2 His mother's very short. [B] 6 Jim's children wear glasses. [ ]
3 My cousin's car is very big. [ ] 7 My brother's wife plays the piano. [ ]
4 Our grandfather's 70 today. [ ] 8 Her name's Christina. [ ]

d Complete the sentences with *whose* or *who's*.

1 ___Whose___ is that bag?
2 ___Who's___ the woman in the red dress?
3 _____ umbrella is this?
4 _____ her boyfriend?
5 _____ the man with the sunglasses?
6 _____ are those keys?
7 _____ your English teacher?
8 _____ headphones are those?

3 PRONUNCIATION the letter o; 's

a Match the sentences 1–4 to the sounds a–d.

1	Th**o**se ph**o**nes are **o**ld.	☐	a ↑ **up**
2	Wh**o** d**o** y**ou** ch**oo**se?	☐	b ☎ **phone**
3	Their s**o**n c**o**mes every M**o**nday.	☐	c 🕐 **clock**
4	That bl**o**nd m**o**del is a d**o**ctor.	☐	d 👢 **boot**

b iChecker Listen and check. Then listen again and repeat the words.

c iChecker Listen to the sentences. Then listen again and repeat.

1 S That**'s** Mark**'s** niece.   They're Kate**'s** parents.

2 Z He**'s** Sandra**'s** husband.   She**'s** Andy**'s** cousin.

3 /IZ/ I'm Grace**'s** boyfriend.   Are you Charles**'s** wife?

4 READING

a Read the article and complete the sentence.

Mason is Kim Kardashian's _____ .

5 LISTENING

iChecker Listen to Jessie showing photos to her friend. How many photos does she show? Then listen again. Write T (true) or F (false).

1 Jessie's sister has a son.   *F*
2 Jessie's sister is short.   ___
3 Jessie's sister plays basketball.   ___
4 The beach in the photo is in Canada.   ___
5 Jessie went to a music festival with her sister.   ___
6 Rosie has blond hair.   ___
7 Rosie sees her boyfriend all the time.   ___
8 Pete is Jessie's boss.   ___

USEFUL WORDS AND PHRASES

Learn these words and phrases.

boyfriend /ˈbɔɪfrɛnd/
celebrity /səˈlɛbrəti/
ex-husband /ɛks ˈhʌzbənd/
girlfriend /ˈgərlfrɛnd/
politician /pɑləˈtɪʃn/
be interested in /bi ˈɪntrəstəd/
private life /ˈpraɪvət laɪf/
the other (person) /ði ˈʌðər/

A Celebrity Family

The Kardashian family is one of the very famous celebrity families in the US. Kim Kardashian is probably the most famous of them.

Kim's mother is Kris. Her father is Robert. Together, they had three daughters, Kim, Khloe, and Kourtney, and a son, Rob. Kris and Robert were divorced in 1990. In 1991, Kris married a famous sports star, Bruce Jenner. Bruce had two sons, Brody and Brandon. Then he had two daughters with Kris, Kendall and Kylie.

Kim's sister Khloe married basketball player Lamar Odom. Kim's other sister, Kourtney, has babies named Mason and Penelope. Kim married basketball player Kris Humphries in 2011, but they were divorced by the end of the year.

Glossary
married = past tense of *marry*
was = past of *is*
were = past of *are*
had = past of *have*

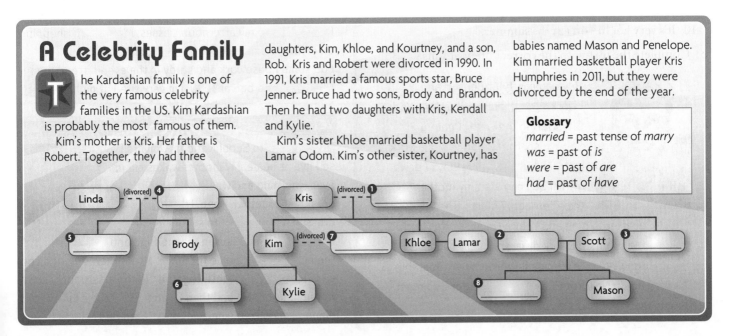

b Read the article again and complete the names in the family tree.

Three o'clock is always too late or too early
for anything you want to do.

Jean-Paul Sartre, French philosopher

4B What a life!

1 GRAMMAR prepositions of time (*at, in, on*) and place (*at, in, to*)

a Write the words in the correct column.

March	~~December 6th~~	~~6:30~~	the winter	Monday	night
the afternoon	noon	Saturday	evening	1984
breakfast	August 21st

in	on	at
March	*December 6th*	*6:30*

b Circle the correct preposition.

1 I take a shower **in** / **on** / **at** the morning.
2 They go on holiday **in** / **on** / **at** August.
3 My sister studies economics **at** / **in** / **to** college.
4 My brother goes to bed **in** / **on** / **at** midnight.
5 Do you work **at** / **in** / **to** a hospital?
6 We have English classes **in** / **on** / **at** Tuesdays and Thursdays.
7 The children have lunch **at** / **in** / **to** school.
8 Tina works **in** / **on** / **at** the weekend.
9 Jack goes **at** / **in** / **to** the gym after work.
10 It's very hot **in** / **on** / **at** the summer.

c Complete the text with the correct prepositions.

"My name is Tyler Benson and I work [1]_____ an office in New York City. During the week, I get up [2]_____ six-thirty. I go [3]_____ work by train, but [4]_____ Fridays I drive my car so I can visit my mother [5]_____ the afternoon. I start work [6]_____ quarter to nine and I have lunch [7]_____ work. [8]_____ the summer, I work different hours because [9]_____ June 15th, we change to the summer timetable. It's very hot in New York City [10]_____ August, so most people go on vacation.

2 VOCABULARY everyday activities

a Circle the action that you usually do first.

1 get up / wake up
2 get dressed / take a shower
3 have lunch / have breakfast
4 go to work / start work
5 go home / get home
6 make dinner / go shopping

b Complete the text with *have*, *go*, or *get*.

A STUDENT'S LIFE IS EASY – OR IS IT?

Many people think that students have a very easy life. We ask two, Elena and Yejoon, about their typical day.

ELENA RAMOS, from São Paulo in Brazil

"I [1] *go* to a college in Texas in the US, so I don't live at home. Every day, I [2]_____ up at 7:30 and I take a shower. I don't have time for breakfast, but I [3]_____ coffee in a cafe before classes start. I [4]_____ lunch at school, and then I [5]_____ to my afternoon classes. I [6]_____ shopping on my way home, so I [7]_____ home late. I do some housework and study in the evening, and then I [8]_____ to bed at 11:30. I'm very tired at night!"

YEJOON KIM, is from Seoul, South Korea

"I [9]_____ to Seoul National University, so I live at home. My mother wakes me up every morning and we [10]_____ breakfast together. Then, I [11]_____ dressed. I [12]_____ to school by bus. I [13]_____ to classes in the morning and then I [14]_____ home for lunch. My mother is a good cook and we [15]_____ lunch together. In the afternoon, I study for an hour or two and then I watch TV. I take a bath after dinner. I'm relaxed when I [16]_____ to bed."

c Match the words to make phrases.

1 have   ☐   a work
2 go   ☐   b emails
3 check   ☐   c dressed
4 do   ☐   d to school
5 get   ☐   e breakfast

3 PRONUNCIATION linking and sentence stress

a Mark the connected words in each sentence.

1 You get up late.
2 I take a shower.
3 We check emails.
4 He has a coffee.
5 She goes home early.
6 They have lunch at work.

b **iChecker** Listen and check. Then listen again and repeat the sentences. Try to connect words.

c **iChecker** Listen and underline the stressed words. Copy the rhythm.

1 I wake up at six.
2 I take a bath.
3 I go to work by bus.
4 I do the housework.
5 I have a pizza for dinner.
6 I go to bed at midnight.

d **iChecker** Listen again and repeat the sentences. Copy the rhythm.

4 LISTENING

a **iChecker** Listen to an interview with Mark. Answer the questions.

1 What does he do? _____
2 Does he like his job? _____
3 When does he work? _____

b **iChecker** Listen again. Number the activities in the order Mark does them.

☐1☐ Mark starts work at 7 p.m.
☐ He goes to bed.
☐ He goes to the gym.
☐ He goes home.
☐ He has a hamburger or a pizza.
☐ He watches TV or checks his emails.
☐ He gets up.
☐ He has breakfast.
☐ He sleeps for eight hours.
☐ He has dinner.
☐ He finishes work.
☐ He takes a shower.

USEFUL WORDS AND PHRASES

Learn these words and phrases.

customers /ˈkʌstəmərz/
everyone /ˈɛvriwʌn/
everything /ˈɛvriθɪŋ/
menu /ˈmɛnyu/
busy /ˈbɪzi/
ready /ˈrɛdi/
a couple of (hours) /ə ˈkʌpl əv/
go back /goʊ ˈbæk/
prepare food /prɪpɛr ˈfud/
enjoy /ɪnˈdʒɔɪ/

4C Short life, long life?

1 GRAMMAR position of adverbs and expressions of frequency

a Complete the *You* column in the chart. Then complete the sentences with a verb and an adverb of frequency.

		Matt	Becky	You
always	✓✓✓✓✓			
usually	✓✓✓✓			
often	✓✓✓			
sometimes	✓✓			
hardly ever	✓			
never	–			
sleep for eight hours		✓✓✓✓	✓✓	
be relaxed		✓✓✓✓✓	✓✓✓	
play sports or exercise		✓✓	–	
eat healthy food		✓✓✓	✓	
be sick		–	✓✓✓✓✓	

1 Matt ___usually sleeps___ for eight hours.
2 He _____ relaxed.
3 He _____ sports or exercises.
4 He _____ healthy food.
5 He _____ sick.

6 Becky _____ for eight hours.
7 She _____ relaxed.
8 She _____ sports and exercises.
9 She _____ healthy food.
10 She _____ sick.

11 I _____ for eight hours.
12 I _____ relaxed.
13 I _____ sports and exercises.
14 I _____ healthy food.
15 I _____ sick.

b Write the adverb of frequency in the correct place in the sentence.

1 Pilots sleep in hotels. (often)
    ___Pilots often sleep in hotels___.
2 The children walk to school. (every day)
    ___The children walk to school every day.___
3 Mike rides his motorcycle to work. (sometimes)
    _____.
4 My sister is late. (never)
    _____.

5 I see my grandparents. (every weekend)
    _____.
6 Ellie drinks coffee. (three times a day)
    _____.
7 I'm hungry. (always)
    _____.
8 We study English. (twice a week)
    _____.

2 VOCABULARY adverbs and expressions of frequency

a Answer the questions.

THE TIME QUIZ

1 How many minutes in an hour? _____
2 How many months in a year? _____
3 How many days in a week? _____
4 How many seconds in a minute? _____
5 How many weeks in a month? _____
6 How many hours in a day? _____
7 How many days in June? _____
8 How many weeks in a year? _____

b Complete the sentences with one or two words.

1 Leo goes to the gym all week and on weekends.
    Leo goes to the gym ___every___ ___day___.
2 Tomo usually takes a vacation in the summer and winter.
    Tomo usually takes a vacation _____ a year.
3 We usually see one new film a month.
    We go to the movie theater _____ a month.
4 Adele doesn't do any homework at all.
    Adele _____ does homework.
5 They have English classes on Mondays, Wednesdays, and Fridays.
    They have English classes _____ _____ a week.
6 My mother goes to the hair salon once a week, on a Friday.
    My mother goes to the hair salon _____ Friday.
7 Sofia walks to work once a year.
    Sofia _____ ever walks to work.
8 I always buy a new pair of sunglasses in the summer.
    I buy a new pair of sunglasses _____ summer.

3 PRONUNCIATION the letter h

a Match the words to their pronunciation. In which word is the *h* not pronounced? _____

1 half [e]   a /hɪr/
2 high [ ]   b /'aʊər/
3 how [ ]   c /haɪ/
4 hour [ ]   d /'həri/
5 hardly [ ]   e /hæf/
6 here [ ]   f /'hæpi/
7 hurry [ ]   g /'hɑrdli/
8 happy [ ]   h /haʊ/

b [iChecker] Listen and check. Then listen again and repeat the words.

4 READING

a Read the interview. What is surprising about Esther Armstrong?

Interview with
Esther Armstrong, 94

Interviewer	How do you spend your day, Esther?
Esther	My day is very normal, really. I get up, I get dressed, I have breakfast. Then I go to work.
Interviewer	What do you do?
Esther	I'm an accountant.
Interviewer	Why do you still work, Esther?
Esther	To have an interest. Also, my job is very exciting.
Interviewer	What time do you start work?
Esther	I start between 9 and 10 every day and I finish at 4 o'clock. It isn't very stressful, really.
Interviewer	What do you usually do after work, Esther?
Esther	I go out for dinner with friends two or three times a week, and we go to the movies or the theater, or to the ballet.
Interviewer	Do you live alone?
Esther	Yes, I do. I have quite a big apartment and someone helps me with the housework for four hours a week. I do everything else myself.
Interviewer	Do you have children, Esther?
Esther	Yes, I do. Both of my daughters live here in New York. One daughter works nearby, and she comes and has lunch with me. And I work with the other daughter, so we eat together two or three times a week, too. I'm very, very happy with my life.

> **Glossary**
> *an accountant* = a person whose job it is to make lists of all the money that people or businesses receive and pay

b Read the interview again. Write T (true) or F (false).

1 Esther thinks her day is normal.   *F*
2 She doesn't like her job.   ___
3 She sometimes starts work at 10 o'clock.   ___
4 She thinks her job is difficult.   ___
5 She often sees friends after work.   ___
6 She lives with one of her children.   ___
7 She never does housework.   ___
8 She has two children.   ___

c Underline five words you don't know. Use your dictionary to look up their meaning and pronunciation.

5 LISTENING

a [iChecker] Listen to a radio program about being healthy. Who does the doctor say is healthy: Marge, Robbie, or Marge and Robbie?

_____

b [iChecker] Listen again. Write T (true) or F (false).

1 Robbie doesn't think he's healthy.   *F*
2 Marge hardly ever eats fast food.   ___
3 Marge always has breakfast.   ___
4 Marge often goes to the gym.   ___
5 Marge goes to bed late.   ___
6 Robbie sometimes has breakfast.   ___
7 Robbie plays soccer three times a week.   ___
8 Robbie sleeps for six hours every night.   ___

> **USEFUL WORDS AND PHRASES**
>
> **Learn these words and phrases.**
>
> hours /'aʊərz/
> minutes /'mɪnəts/
> seconds /'sɛkəndz/
> teenager /'tineɪdʒər/
> healthy (*opposite* unhealthy) /'hɛlθi/
> normally /'nɔrməli/
> relax /rɪ'læks/
> be in a hurry /bi ɪn ə 'həri/
> social life /'soʊʃl laɪf/
> spend time /spɛnd 'taɪm/

[iChecker] [TESTS] FILE 4

5A Are you the next American Idol?

1 GRAMMAR *can / can't*

a Write a sentence for each picture with *can / can't*.

1 *They can't sing* .

2 _____ .

3 _____ .

4 _____ .

5 _____ .

b Write a question with *you* for each picture. Then write your answer: *Yes, I can.* or *No, I can't.*

				Your answer
1	*Can*	you	*sing* ?	_____ .
2	____	you	_____ ?	_____ .
3	____	you	_____ ?	_____ .
4	____	you	_____ ?	_____ .
5	____	you	_____ ?	_____ .

c Match sentences 1–6 to a–f.

1 Can you help me with my homework? I [c]
2 Can you give me my glasses? I [ ]
3 Can you call my mom? I [ ]
4 Can you speak more slowly? I [ ]
5 Can you make dinner for 8:30? I [ ]
6 Can you tell me your name again? I [ ]

a can't come before then.
b can't see.
c ~~can't do it.~~
d can't find my cell phone.
e can't understand you.
f can't remember it.

d Write a sentence with *can* or *can't* for each picture.

1 You ___*can cross*___ now.

2 I _____ now.

3 Dr. Atkins _____ you now.

4 We _____ here!

2 VOCABULARY verb phrases

a Complete the crossword with the correct verb.

Clues across →

Clues down ↓

Bill? Tony?

Tom!

b Complete the sentences.

| buy ~~find~~ hear help look for play run talk |

1 He can't __*find*__ any parking spaces. There are a lot of cars.
2 I often _____ chess with my nephew. He's very good.
3 Please _____ me. I can't open the door.
4 I _____ most of my clothes from Zara.
5 I want to _____ in the Boston Marathon this year.
6 Hi, this is Paul. Can you _____ me?
7 I don't understand this. I need to _____ to the teacher.
8 Where are my keys? Can you _____ them?

3 PRONUNCIATION sentence stress

a (iChecker) Listen and repeat the sentences. Stress the **bold** words.

1 A **Can** you **speak German**?
  B **Yes**, I **can**.
2 I **can't find** the **keys**.
3 **She** can **sing**.
4 **Where** can I **buy** a **newspaper**?
5 A **Can** your **father cook**?
  B **No**, he **can't**.
6 My **sister can't swim**.

b Write the words in the chart.

| are bad can card far fat |
| have park stamp start |

æ cat	*bad*	_____
	_____	_____
ɑr car	*are*	_____
	_____	_____

c (iChecker) Listen and check. Then listen again and repeat the words.

4 LISTENING

(iChecker) Listen to the dialogues and choose a, b, or c.

1 When can they go to the swimming pool?
  a On Saturday morning.
  b On Saturday afternoon.
  c On Sunday afternoon.
2 Where can the man park?
  a Outside the hospital.
  b Outside the restaurant.
  c Outside the movie theater.
3 When can she help her brother?
  a This morning.
  b This afternoon.
  c This evening.
4 Why can't they send the postcard?
  a They don't have a pen.
  b They don't have the address.
  c They don't have a stamp.
5 Why can't they go in?
  a He can't open the door.
  b He can hear his boss.
  c He can't find his keys.

USEFUL WORDS AND PHRASES

Learn these words and phrases.

audience /ˈɔdiəns/
concerts /ˈkɑnsərts/
entrance /ˈɛntrəns/
judges /ˈdʒʌdʒɪz/
late (*opposite* early) /leɪt/
nervous /ˈnərvəs/
a hit record /ə hɪt ˈrɛkərd/
parking lot /ˈpɑrkɪŋ lɑt/
Good luck! /gʊd ˈlʌk/
It's your turn now. /ɪts ˈyər tərn naʊ/

31

5B Love your neighbors

1 VOCABULARY verb phrases

Complete the text with these verbs in the simple present.

argue ~~shout~~ bark cry talk have
have play play

My neighbors are very noisy. A young couple with a baby and a dog live upstairs. They aren't happy together, so they [1] *shout* all the time. Their dog [2] _____ when they aren't at home, and their baby [3] _____ when they are. An old couple lives downstairs. They can't hear, so they always [4] _____ the TV on very loud. They [5] _____ loudly because the TV is loud, and they [6] _____ a lot about which shows to watch. Some students live next door. They all [7] _____ musical instruments and they aren't very good! Every night, they [8] _____ noisy parties and [9] _____ very loud music. I want a new apartment or some new neighbors!

2 GRAMMAR present continuous

a Order the words to make sentences.

1 sister's / My / exams / for / studying / her.
  My sister's studying for her exams .

2 with / staying / week / her / friends / this / are / Sarah's
  _____

3 tonight / party / We / a / aren't / having
  _____

4 I'm / cup / coffee / drinking / a / the / of / kitchen / in
  _____

5 for / looking / job / is / a / Marco / Why
  _____ ?

6 because / aren't / They / jogging / today / cold / it's / too
  _____

7 computer / Are / using / you / the
  _____ ?

8 soccer / Is / park / Adam / playing / in / the
  _____ ?

b Complete the dialogue.

A What [1] *are you doing* , (you / do) Andy?
B [2] _____ (I / make) the coffee. Why?
A I can hear a noise. It's people's voices.
B I know. That's the couple upstairs.
A [3] _____ (they / argue)?
B No, [4] _____ (they / not shout). It's the TV. They're very old, so they can't hear it. [5] _____ (they / watch) a movie.
A Oh. What's that music? Is it a party?
B It's the boy next door. [6] _____ (he / not have) a party!
  [7] _____ (he / listen) to music. He likes heavy metal.
A Your apartment is very noisy, Andy.
B I know. [8] _____ (I / look for) a new one!

c Look at the picture on page 33. What are the people doing? Complete 1–9 with a verb or verb phrase in the present continuous.

1 The woman *'s talking on her cell phone.* .
2 The couple _____ .
3 The children _____ .
4 The woman _____ .
5 The baby _____ .
6 The dog _____ .
7 The boy _____ .
8 The girl _____ .

3 PRONUNCIATION /ŋ/

a  Listen and repeat the words.

ŋ singer	arguing barking crying having playing shouting studying talking

b Circle the word with /ŋ/ in each pair.

1	sing	dance
2	pink	brown
3	thin	long
4	aunt	uncle
5	drink	find
6	France	England
7	young	blond
8	think	want

c iChecker Listen and check. Then listen again and repeat the words.

4 LISTENING

iChecker Listen to four speakers talking about problems with their neighbors. Match the speakers to the problems. There are two problems you don't need to use.

Speaker 1 ☐   A   They argue a lot.
Speaker 2 ☐   B   Their dogs bark.
Speaker 3 ☐   C   They have noisy parties.
Speaker 4 ☐   D   They have the TV on very loud.
                E   Their baby cries.
                F   They play musical instruments.

USEFUL WORDS AND PHRASES

Learn these words and phrases.

furniture /ˈfərnɪtʃər/
neighbors /ˈneɪbərz/
noise /nɔɪz/
noisy /ˈnɔɪzi/
strict /strɪkt/
upstairs (*opposite* downstairs) /ʌpˈstɛrz/
now /naʊ/
complain /kəmˈpleɪn/
apartment building /əˈpɑrtmənt bɪldɪŋ/
washing machine /ˈwɑʃɪŋ məʃin/

I'm leaving because the weather is too good.
I hate London when it's not raining.

Groucho Marx, American actor

5C Sun and the City

1 GRAMMAR simple present or present continuous?

a (Circle) the correct form.

1 **A** What are you doing here?
   B I'm on vacation. **I sightsee** / (**I'm sightseeing**) .

2 **A** Can you talk?
   B No. **I have dinner** / **I'm having dinner** right now.

3 **A** Where **do they usually go** / **are they usually going** on vacation?
   B To Florida.

4 **A** How often does your husband go abroad?
   B **He travels** / **He's traveling** to Asia four times a year.

5 **A** What **does your friend do** / **is your friend doing**?
   B She's a travel guide.

6 **A** **Do you work** / **Are you working** this week?
   B No. I'm on vacation.

7 **A** What time does the museum close?
   B **It closes** / **It's closing** at 6 p.m., I think.

8 **A** **Does it rain** / **Is it raining** today?
   B No. It's hot and sunny.

b Complete the sentences. Use the simple present or present continuous.

1 My parents ___don't like___ (not like) their hotel.
2 They _____ (argue) about money all the time.
3 I'm 18 now, so I _____ (learn) to drive. My father _____ (teach) me.
4 When _____ you usually _____ (go) to the gym?
5 My brother _____ (go out) almost every night.
6 The sun _____ (not shine) today. It's quite cold.
7 _____ you _____ (use) your computer right now? I _____ (want) to check something on the Internet.
8 My sister _____ (love) ice skating but she _____ (not do) it very often.

2 VOCABULARY the weather and seasons

a Write the seasons in the correct order.

___winter___ , _____ , _____ , _____

b Complete the sentences with words in the box. What's the weather like?

cloudy cold foggy ~~hot~~ raining snowing sunny windy

1 It's ___hot___ .

2 It's _____.

3 It's _____.

4 It's _____.

5 It's _____.

6 It's _____.

7 It's _____.

8 It's _____.

3 PRONUNCIATION places in New York City

a Underline the stressed syllable.

1 Ro|cke|fe|ller Cen|ter
2 Yan|kee Sta|di|um
3 E|llis Is|land
4 St. Pa|trick's Ca|the|dral
5 Grand Cen|tral Ter|mi|nal
6 the Broo|klyn Bridge
7 the Sta|tue of Li|ber|ty
8 Wa|shing|ton Square Park

b **iChecker** Listen and check. Then listen again and repeat the words.

4 READING

Read the guidebook extract about things to do in Denver. Write T (true) or F (false).

1 The Molly Brown House Museum is outside the city. _F_
2 Molly Brown is famous because she is an actress. ___
3 You can see clothes from one of Molly's trips. ___
4 You can see the city very well from Red Rocks Park. ___
5 You can use a camera in the park. ___
6 The theater at Red Rocks Park is very small. ___
7 Glennwood Hot Springs is in the center of Denver. ___
8 One pool is big. ___
9 The water is different in the summer and the winter. ___

5 LISTENING

iChecker Listen to the descriptions of places to visit in Victoria, British Columbia and write the number of the tour.

Which tour do you need to take if you want to…?

A see some old Asian art ☐
B learn about insects ☐
C see some animals and play sports ☐
D listen to music ☐ 1
E have a drink and take a swim ☐
F see a place that is famous because of a movie ☐
G see a lot of books ☐
H learn about a famous Canadian ☐

What to do in DENVER

1 WHEN IT'S RAINING Go to the Molly Brown House Museum

The Molly Brown House Museum is a big, beautiful house on 1340 Pennsylvania Avenue in the center of Denver. Molly Brown is world famous because she was on the *Titanic*. You can take a tour of Molly's house. You can see interesting exhibitions, including clothes and other items from her trip on the *Titantic*. If the sun comes out, you can walk in Molly's yard or sit in her gardens.

2 WHEN THE SUN IS SHINING Go to Red Rocks Park

Red Rocks Park is a mountain park in southwest Denver with excellent views of the city. The park gets its name from big red rocks that are special to this area. The rocks are over 290 million years old. You can walk around the park and take pictures of famous rocks like Creation Rock, Ship Rock, or Stage Rock. Or, you can go to a concert and listen to bands like U2 and Coldplay. The theater can seat almost 10,000 people.

3 WHEN IT'S COLD Go to Glennwood Hot Springs

Glennwood Hot Springs is a hotel with an outdoor pool that's open all year. It isn't in Devner, but it's nearby in the Rocky Mountains. The hotel has two pools. One is a small pool. The other pool is 405 feet long! The water in the big pool is always 90° F, even in January! If you don't like to swim in the cold, visit the spa or enjoy lunch at the restaurant.

USEFUL WORDS AND PHRASES

Learn these words and phrases.

building /ˈbɪldɪŋ/
guidebook /ˈɡaɪdbʊk/
monument /ˈmɑnyəmənt/
parks /pɑrks/
statue /ˈstætʃu/
enormous /ɪˈnɔrməs/
fascinating /ˈfæsəneɪtɪŋ/
wonderful /ˈwʌndərfl/
including /ɪnˈkludɪŋ/
open-air swimming pool /oʊpən ɛr ˈswɪmɪŋ pul/

iChecker **TESTS** FILE 5

1 VOCABULARY clothes

Write the words.

1 _a jacket_   5 _____
2 _____   6 _____
3 _____   7 _____
4 _____   8 _____

2 BUYING CLOTHES

Complete the missing words in the dialogue.

A Can I ¹**h**___ you?
B Yes. What ²**s**_____ is this T-shirt?
A It's a medium. What size do you need?
B I need a ³**l**_____.
A Here you ⁴**a**_____.
B Thanks. Where can I try it on?
A The ⁵**f**_____ rooms are over there.
B ⁶**Th**_____ you.
A How is it?
B It's fine. How ⁷**m**_____ is it?
A It's $15.99.

3 SOCIAL ENGLISH

Match the words to make Social English phrases.

1 It's so | d | a way!
2 Right | | b wrong?
3 Don't | | c be silly!
4 Wait | | d ~~cool!~~
5 I have to | | e fun!
6 Have | | f now.
7 What's | | g go.
8 No | | h a minute.

4 READING

a Read the article. Match the questions A–D to paragraphs 1–4.

A What can you do there? | 1 |
B How do you get there? | |
C Where can you eat there? | |
D What time does it open? | |

Shopping in the US

One of the best places to shop in the US these days is at the Fashion Island mall in Newport Beach, California—this open-air shopping mall is the nicest of its kind in California.

1 Customers at Fashion Island can buy fashion, food, home, and beauty products from more than 150 different stores. There are three huge department stores and a large supermarket. It has a seven-screen movie theater, four hotels, and a view of the Pacific Ocean.

2 Fashion Island has more than 35 different restaurants and food bars. There are take-out restaurants and sit-down restaurants, including Hawaiian food and a bakery that sells vegan desserts and salads. Many of the restaurants stay open after the stores close.

3 Most of the stores in the shopping mall open from 10 a.m. to 9 p.m. during the week, and from 10 a.m. to 7 p.m. on Saturday. The opening hours on Sunday are from 11 a.m. to 6 p.m. The restaurants close around midnight and the movie theater closes at 11 p.m.

4 Fashion Island has more than 6,000 parking spaces and three valet parking stations. You can get to this shopping mall by public transportation, too. Fashion Island is only one-half mile from the Pacific Coast Highway and about 5 minutes from John Wayne Airport.

b Guess the meaning of the highlighted words. Check the meaning and pronunciation in your dictionary.

6A Reading in English

1 GRAMMAR object pronouns

a Complete the chart.

Subject pronouns	Object pronouns
I	¹ *me*
²	you
he	³
she	⁴
⁵	it
we	⁶
⁷	you
they	⁸

b Complete the sentences with object pronouns.

1 My sister has a new friend. She's on vacation with ___her___ right now.
2 Can you hear _____, or do I need to shout?
3 This book is very exciting. I'm really enjoying _____.
4 He works near his wife's office. He has lunch with _____ every day.
5 Are you at home? Can I call _____ later?
6 Alberto doesn't live with his parents, but he talks to _____ once a week.
7 Excuse me, we have a problem. Can you help _____?
8 I can't find my bag. Can you see _____?
9 These shoes are new. Do you like _____?
10 Where's Charlie? I want to talk to _____.

c Complete the text with these words.

he   her   her   him   him   she   them   they

Lily is worried about her boyfriend, Jamie. She calls
¹ ___him___ every day, but he doesn't call ² _____.
When she wants to talk to Jamie, ³ _____ always says
he's busy. She waits for ⁴ _____ after work, but he's
usually with some friends. Jamie's friends don't like Lily,
and she doesn't like ⁵ _____. Lily says hello, but
⁶ _____ won't look at her. Now she knows that Jamie
doesn't love ⁷ _____. But she's happy because she
knows that ⁸ _____ can find a new boyfriend.

2 VOCABULARY phone language

Complete the dialogues with these words.

answer   It's   message
Press   there   this   wrong

1 **A** Hello. Is Marta ___there___?
  B No, I'm sorry. She isn't.
2 **A** What number is this?
  B _____ 917-555-9832.
3 **A** The phone's ringing.
  B Can you _____ it, please?
4 **A** Hello, is this Sophie?
  B No, I'm sorry, _____ is Grace.
5 **A** How do I end this call?
  B _____ the red button.
6 **A** This is 714-555-3822.
  B I'm very sorry. It's the _____ number.
7 **A** I'm sorry, the manager is in a meeting.
  B Oh. Can you give him a _____?

3 PRONUNCIATION /aɪ/, /i/, and /ɪ/

a **iChecker** Listen and repeat the sentences. Stress the **bold** words.

1 **Call** me **tonight**.
2 **Can** you **help** us?
3 **Don't listen** to **her**.
4 **See** you **later**.
5 **I don't like** them.
6 **Don't think** about it.
7 **Give it** to **him**.

b (Circle) the word with a different sound.

fish	1	him	live	nice	fish	4	these his ring
tree	2	she	this	meet	tree	5	we leave it
bike	3	me	I	my	bike	6	smile niece buy

c iChecker Listen and check. Then listen and repeat the words.

4 READING

Read some more of *Sally's Phone* and answer the questions.

1 Who's Katharine? _____

2 What does Louise suggest to Sally?

_____

3 Why doesn't Paul know his phone number?

_____

4 Who tells him what his number is? _____

Sally's Phone

Sally talks to Claire and Louise.
"I have a message for Paul – but who's Paul? Do you know a Paul, Claire?" she asks.
"No. What's the message?" Claire asks.
"It's his sister Katharine's birthday, and she's having a party tonight. Do you think it's a wrong number?"
"Yes, I think it is," Claire says.
"Hey, Sally!" Louise says. "Put on your red skirt and go to the party. Forget Andrew!"
Paul talks to a friend at work.
"This is Sally's phone – and Sally has my phone."
"But who is Sally?"
"I don't know," says Paul.
"Why don't you call her?"
"What's my number?" Paul asks. "I don't know my number."
"Why not?"
"Because I never call my number!"
Paul calls his mother.
"Mom, what's the number of my phone?"
"Why do you want your phone number, Paul?"
"Because Sally has my phone."
"Who's Sally?" his mother asks.
"I don't know, but she has my phone, and I have her phone."
"I don't understand."
"I know," says Paul. "It doesn't matter. Do you have my number?"
"Here it is. 0781 644834."
"Thanks, Mom."

5 LISTENING

iChecker Listen to the phone conversation. Choose a or b.

1 Who does Holly want to talk to?
  a Beth   b Emily
2 Where is Emily?
  a at home   b out
3 Where is Holly's bag?
  a in Emily's car   b in Emily's house
4 What is Holly's phone number?
  a 606-555-4923   b 606-555-9423
5 What does Beth give Emily?
  a the message   b the phone
6 Which keys are in Holly's bag?
  a her car keys   b her apartment keys
7 Who is Holly with?
  a a neighbor   b a friend
8 Where do Holly and Emily meet?
  a at Holly's house   b in a cafe

USEFUL WORDS AND PHRASES

Learn these words and phrases.

voice /vɔɪs/
fall /fɔl/
happening /ˈhæpənɪŋ/
ring /rɪŋ/
smile /smaɪl/
give a message (to somebody) /gɪv ə ˈmɛsɪdʒ/
pick up /ˈpɪk ʌp/
press the button /prɛs ðə ˈbʌtn/
put down /ˈpʊt daʊn/
It's the wrong number. /ɪts ðə rɔŋ ˈnʌmbər/

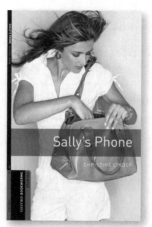

Extract from Oxford Bookworms Library Starter:
Sally's Phone by Christine Lindop © Oxford University Press 2008.
Reproduced by Permission.
ISBN 978-0-19-423426-9

6B Times we love

1 GRAMMAR *like + (verb + -ing)*

a Write the verb + *-ing* form of the verbs in the box in the
correct column.

buy come draw find get have give run stop
swim take wait

verb + *-ing*	e + *-ing*	double consonant + *-ing*
buying		

b Look at the chart and complete the sentences.

☺☺ = love
☺ = like
😐 = don't mind
☹ = don't like
☹☹ = hate

	William	Amanda
dance at parties	☹☹	☺☺
do housework	😐	☹☹
drive at night	☺	☹
sit in cafés	😐	☺
swim in the ocean	☺☺	☹
watch soccer	☹	☺☺

1 William ___*hates dancing*___ at parties.
    Amanda _____ at parties.
2 William _____ housework.
    Amanda _____ housework.
3 William _____ at night.
    Amanda _____ at night.
4 William _____ in cafés.
    Amanda _____ in cafés.
5 William _____ in the ocean.
    Amanda _____ in the ocean.
6 William _____ soccer.
    Amanda _____ soccer.

2 VOCABULARY the date; ordinal numbers

a Continue the series.

1 September, October, ___*November*___, ___*December*___
2 May, June, _____, _____
3 January, February, _____, _____
4 spring, summer, _____, _____
5 first, second, _____, _____
6 sixth, seventh, _____, _____
7 eighteenth, nineteenth, _____, _____

b Complete the chart.

1/1   2/14   7/4   10/31   ~~5/1~~

Day	Date	You say...
May Day	5/1	*May first*
Halloween		
New Year's Day		
US Independence Day		
Valentine's Day		

3 PRONUNCIATION consonant clusters; saying the date

a Underline the stressed syllable in the multisyllable words.

1 January   7 July
2 February   8 August
3 March   9 September
4 April   10 October
5 May   11 November
6 June   12 December

b **iChecker** Listen and check. Then listen and
repeat the words.

c **iChecker** Listen and repeat the dates.

1 4 / 3	6 6 / 14
2 12 / 26	7 2 / 1
3 5 / 11	8 11 / 7
4 1 / 5	9 10 / 22
5 3 / 18	10 7 / 12

4 READING

Read the article about important dates in the US and find the answers to the questions. Write **A**, **B**, **C**, or **D**.

On which day or days…?

1 do some people watch sports on TV? [D]
2 do people think about a man who helped others [ ]
3 do people help the earth [ ]
4 do people go to work [ ] [ ]
5 do people hear or read stories that aren't true [ ]
6 do some people walk outside in big groups [ ]

US dates to remember

A April Fool's Day is on April 1st. It isn't a national holiday, but it's a day when people play jokes on friends and family. Some good jokes are on the Internet, in the newspapers, or on TV—for example, one year on the Internet, a compnay that sells glasses put an advertisement for dog sunglasses on its website. Many people believed it was true.

B Earth Day isn't a national US holiday, but it is day the US and the rest of the world thinks about the earth and how to help it. People do things like clean up parks, ride their bikes, or plant trees. The first Earth Day was in 1970.

C Martin Luther King, Jr. Day is a US national holiday. On the third Monday in January, Americans remember Dr. King and his work helping Americans in the 1960s. Most schools and some businesses close for the day. There are also parades and talks to celebrate Dr. King.

D Thanksgiving is a US national holiday on the fourth Thursday of November. A traditional Thanksgiving activity is cooking a turkey and eating a big meal with family and friends. After the meal, many people watch American football on TV or sit around the table and tell stories or play games.

5 LISTENING

a **iChecker** Listen to four speakers talk about their favorite times of year. Match the speakers to the seasons.

Speaker 1	spring
Speaker 2	fall
Speaker 3	winter
Speaker 4	summer

b **iChecker** Listen again. Match the speakers to the activities they enjoy doing at that time of year.

Speaker 1 [ ]
Speaker 2 [ ]
Speaker 3 [ ]
Speaker 4 [ ]

a walking
b planning
c taking photos
d traveling

USEFUL WORDS AND PHRASES

Learn these words and phrases.

birthday /ˈbərθdeɪ/
asleep /əˈslip/
depressing /dɪˈprɛsɪŋ/
outside (*opposite* inside) /aʊtˈsaɪd/
hate /heɪt/
in a good mood /ɪn ə gʊd ˈmud/
When's your birthday? /wɛnz yər ˈbərθdeɪ/

Ah, music. A magic beyond all we do here!

J.K. Rowling, British author

6C Music is changing their lives

1 GRAMMAR review: *be* or *do*?

a Complete the sentences with the correct form of *be* or *do*.

1 What ___*are*___ you listening to?
2 Which instrument _____ you play?
3 The singer _____ Spanish. She's Argentinian.
4 I _____ buy CDs. All my music is on my iPod.
5 We _____ watching a movie. We're watching the news.
6 _____ your friend like reggae?
7 Which song _____ your brother downloading?
8 He _____ sing in a group. He's a solo artist.
9 They _____ go to concerts because they're too expensive.
10 _____ you a member of a fan club?

b Rewrite the sentences as questions.

1 They listen to music online.
   Do they listen to music online _____?
2 Bai sings karaoke.
   _____?
3 She's singing in the shower.
   _____?
4 That guitar's expensive.
   _____?
5 They go to a lot of musicals.
   _____?
6 I'm waiting in the right place.
   _____?
7 Kathy likes reggae.
   _____?
8 You go dancing on the weekend.
   _____?
9 He listens to classical music when he's stressed.
   _____?
10 They're in an orchestra.
   _____?

2 VOCABULARY music

a Complete the words.

1 Rihanna is an R*&B* singer from Barbados.
2 Kings of Leon is an American **r**_____ band.
3 Black Eyed Peas is a famous **h**_____ **h**_____ group.
4 Iron Maiden is an English **h**_____ **m**_____ band.
5 John Lee Hooker is famous for **b**_____ music.
6 Bach and Beethoven are two German composers of **c**_____ **m**_____.
7 Jennifer Lopez is a popular singer of **L**_____ music.
8 Many **r**_____ musicians are from Jamaica.
9 Jamie Cullum plays modern **j**_____.

41

b Complete the sentences with the words in the box.

| concert | go dancing | download | fan club |
| karaoke | lyrics | music channels | online |

1 My friends and I often __*go dancing*__ on a Saturday night.
2 My sister loves Green Day and she's a member of their _____.
3 I _____ new music onto my MP3 player almost every day.
4 My children love watching _____, especially MTV.
5 When she's using her laptop, she often listens to music _____.
6 I like the song, but I don't understand the _____.
7 Many Japanese people love singing _____.
8 Would you like to come to a _____ tonight? I have two tickets for Michael Bublé

3 PRONUNCIATION /y/

a (Circle) the word which doesn't have /y/.

y
yacht

1	use	beautiful	umbrella
2	young	journalist	yellow
3	nurse	use	music
4	musician	lunch	usually
5	January	university	summer

b iChecker Listen and check. Then listen and repeat the words.

4 LISTENING

iChecker Listen to the dialogues and choose a, b, or c.

1 Raul thinks reggae is…
   a loud.
   b slow.
   c great.
2 The people who sing on the woman's favorite CD are…
   a a classical choir.
   b a rock band.
   c actors.
3 Wendy usually listens to music…
   a online.
   b on CDs.
   c on the radio.
4 The second man really likes…
   a Rihanna.
   b Beyoncé.
   c Justin Bieber.
5 John…the song.
   a likes
   b doesn't mind
   c hates

USEFUL WORDS AND PHRASES

Learn these words and phrases.

a band /ə bænd/
conductor /kən'dʌktər/
karaoke /kæri'oʊki/
orchestra /'ɔrkəstrə/
soundtrack /'saʊndtræk/
awful /'ɔfl/
fantastic /fæn'tæstɪk/
be a fan (of…) /bi ə 'fæn (əv)/
Be a member (of…) /bi ə 'mɛmbər/
download music /'daʊnloʊd 'myuzɪk/
go dancing /goʊ 'dænsɪŋ/

iChecker TESTS FILE 6

My life is a simple thing that would interest nobody.
It is a known fact that I was born, and that is all that is necessary.

Albert Einstein, German scientist

7A At the National Portrait Gallery

1 GRAMMAR simple past of *be*: was / were

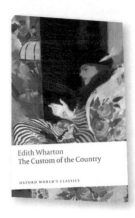

a Complete the sentences with *was*, *were*, *wasn't*, or *weren't*.

> **A** Who's that?
> **B** It's Edith Wharton.
> **A** Why [1] _was_ she famous?
> **B** She [2] _____ a writer.
> **A** [3] _____ she Canadian?
> **B** No, she [4] _____.
> She [5] _____ American. She [6] _____ born in New York City in 1862.
> **A** And [7] _____ she married?
> **B** Yes, she [8] _____.

b Write questions and answers.

1 Alexander Graham Bell / sportsman? ✗

   Was Alexander Graham Bell a sportsman ?
   No, he wasn't .

2 Richard Burton and Elizabeth Taylor / actors? ✓

   Were Richard Burton and Elizabeth Taylor actors ?
   Yes, they were .

3 Jorge Luis Borges / writer? ✓

   _____?
   _____.

4 The Beatles / from the US? ✗

   _____?
   _____.

5 Robert Frost / politician? ✗

   _____?
   _____.

6 I.M. Pei / composer? ✗

   _____?
   _____.

7 Sofia Vergara / born / Columbia? ✓

   _____?
   _____.

8 Frank Sinatra / singer? ✓

   _____?
   _____.

9 J.R.R. Tolkien and C.S. Lewis / painters? ✗

   _____?
   _____.

10 Michael Jackson / born / Britain? ✗

   _____?
   _____.

c Complete the dialogues with present or past forms of *be*.

1 **A** What day _is_ it today?
  B Monday. Yesterday _was_ Sunday.

2 **A** Hi. _____ your sister at home?
  B No, she _____. She _____ here this morning, but now she _____ at work.

3 **A** I can't find my keys. Where _____ they?
  B I don't know. They _____ on your desk this morning.

4 **A** Where _____ your new friend from?
  B He _____ born in the US, but his parents _____ born in Singapore.

5 **A** Why _____ your boss angry yesterday?
  B Because I _____ very late for work.

2 VOCABULARY word formation

a Make professions from these words. Use *a* or *an*.

1 invent   *an inventor*
2 write   _____
3 dance   _____
4 compose   _____
5 music   _____
6 paint   _____
7 business   _____
8 act   _____
9 science   _____
10 sail   _____

b Underline the stressed syllables, e.g. *an inventor*.

c Practice saying the words in **a**.

d Complete the sentences with *was / were* and a noun from **a**.

1 Francis Drake   *was a sailor*   .
2 Beethoven and Mozart   *were composers*   .
3 James Dean _____ .
4 Galileo _____ .
5 Freddie Mercury _____ .
6 The Wright brothers _____ .
7 F. Scott Fitzgerald _____ .
8 Howard Hughes _____ .
9 Degas and Toulouse-Lautrec _____ .

3 PRONUNCIATION sentence stress

iChecker Listen and repeat the conversation.

A Who was Aaron Copland?
B He was a composer.
A Was he British?
B No, he wasn't. He was American.
A When was he born?
B He was born in 1900.
A Were his parents composers?
B No, they weren't.

4 LISTENING

a iChecker Listen to a radio program about the greatest Americans o all time. Number the people in the order they come on the list.

Martin Luther King, Jr.   George Washington   Ben Franklin

Abraham Lincoln   Ronald Reagan

b iChecker Listen again. Write T (true) or F (false).

1 Ben Franklin was a young newspaper owner.   *T*
2 George Washington was born on February 12, 1732.   ___
3 He was 76 when he died.   ___
4 Martin Luther King, Jr. was born on January 15th, 1929.   ___
5 He was young when he died.   ___
6 Abraham Lincoln was a painter.   ___
7 He was 56 when he died.   ___
8 The greatest American of all time was a singer.   ___

USEFUL WORDS AND PHRASES

Learn these words and phrases.

the (16th) century /ðə ˈsɛntʃəri/
killed /kɪld/
between (1816 and 1820) /bɪˈtwin/
be against (something) /bi əˈgɛnst/
be in love (with someone) /bi ɪn ˈlʌv/

7B Chelsea girls

1 GRAMMAR simple past: regular verbs

a Complete the sentences with a regular verb in the simple past, first in the affirmative and then in the negative.

---
book   download   listen   ~~miss~~   play   study   watch   work
---

1 Yesterday I ___missed___ my bus, but I ___didn't miss___ my train.

2 We _____ to the news, but we _____ to the weather.

3 My parents _____ French at school, but they _____ Spanish or Japanese.

4 My sister _____ the movie with me, but she _____ the soccer game.

5 The secretary _____ a table for lunch, but she _____ a taxi.

6 I _____ some music onto my laptop, but I _____ any movies.

7 The salesperson _____ last Saturday, but she _____ on Sunday.

8 My brother _____ tennis at school, but he _____ basketball.

b Order the words to make questions.

1 you / did / night / TV / What / on / last / watch?
A ___What did you watch on TV last night___?
B I watched the news.

2 did / game / the / time / end / What
A _____?
B At six o'clock.

3 your / presents / birthday / like / you / Did
A _____?
B Yes, I did. They were great!

4 did / college / your / in / brother / What / study
A _____?
B Modern Languages.

5 parents / your / arrive / late / Did
A _____?
B No, they didn't. They were early.

6 Brazil / your / in / friends / did / Where / live
A _____?
B Rio de Janeiro.

7 of / you / Did / at / the / cry / movie / end / the
A _____?
B Yes, I did. It was very sad.

8 time / work / did / What / arrive / Luisa / yesterday / at
A _____?
B At ten o'clock.

c Complete the questions and answers.

1990   1997   ~~1998~~   2001   2004   2007   2009

When did it happen?

1 when / the Akashi-Kaikyo Bridge / open
When did the Akashi-Kaikyo Bridge open _____?
It opened in ___1998___ .

2 when / Michael Jackson / die
_____?
He died in _____ .

3 when / Facebook / start
_____?
It started in _____ .

4 when / Princess Diana / die
_____?
She died in _____ .

5 when / the first tourist / travel into space
_____?
It traveled into space in _____ .

6 when / iPhones / first appear
_____?
They appeared in _____ .

7 when / Tim Berners-Lee / create the World Wide Web
_____?
He created it in _____ .

2 VOCABULARY past time expressions

Circle the correct answer.

1 I chatted with my friends for an hour **last night** / **yesterday night**.
2 My girlfriend finished college **ago two years** / **two years ago**.
3 They traveled abroad **last month** / **the last month**.
4 Did you call me **last morning** / **yesterday morning**?
5 It stopped raining **two hours ago** / **two ago hours**.
6 My brother worked in the city **last July** / **the last July**.
7 We watched that movie **before two weeks** / **two weeks ago**.
8 David booked the tickets **yesterday afternoon** / **last afternoon**.
9 Steve was born **in 1990** / **on 1990**.
10 I played golf **the day yesterday before** / **the day before yesterday**.

3 PRONUNCIATION -ed endings

a **iChecker** Listen to the words. Underline the word where -ed is pronounced /ɪd/.

1 booked	checked	wanted	walked
2 painted	arrived	finished	traveled
3 asked	waited	looked	stopped
4 called	played	chatted	listened
5 missed	watched	cooked	started
6 followed	decided	lived	relaxed

b **iChecker** Listen again and repeat the words.

4 READING

a Read the article and choose the best title.

1 The wrong match
2 The wrong destination
3 The wrong player

b Read the article again and answer the questions.

1 How old was Bojana when the incident happened?
2 Where was the tennis tournament?
3 How did she travel to Carlsbad?
4 Where did Bojana travel to first?
5 When did she arrive at the tournament?
6 Who did she play in her first match?
7 Did she win?

5 LISTENING

a **iChecker** Listen to four speakers describing bad trips. How did they travel (e.g., by car, etc.)?

1 _____ 3 _____
2 _____ 4 _____

b **iChecker** Listen again and match the speakers 1–4 to the sentences a–d.

Speaker 1 ☐
Speaker 2 ☐
Speaker 3 ☐
Speaker 4 ☐

A A stranger helped me.
B Someone in my family helped me.
C I started my trip twice.
D I didn't arrive at my destination.

USEFUL WORDS AND PHRASES

Learn these words and phrases.

GPS /dʒi pi 'ɛs/
surprised /sər'praɪzd/
arrive /ə'raɪv/
cry /kraɪ/
miss /mɪs/
text /tɛkst/
travel /'trævl/
country house /kʌntri 'haʊs/

Serbian tennis player Bojana Jovanovski was only 19 when she played in the San Diego Open. However, she almost missed the tournament. Her first match was in Carlsbad, California, so her agent booked a seat for her and gave her the ticket to Carlsbad. It was a long trip because Bojana needed to take three different planes. When she finally arrived in Carlsbad, she was surprised to find that the airport was empty. She waited for 15 minutes and then called Tournament Transportation. The problem was that Bojana was in Carlsbad, New Mexico and the transportation service was in Carlsbad, California where the tournament was. So, Bojana stayed in New Mexico for the night and then traveled to Carlsbad, California the next morning. She arrived only 30 minutes before the start of her match with the Italian player Roberta Vinci. Unfortunately, the day finished badly for Bojana because she lost the match 3-6, 6-4, 6-1. After that, she just wanted to go home!

Never be the first to arrive at a party or the last to go home, and never, ever be both.

Anonymous

7C A night to remember

1 GRAMMAR simple past: irregular verbs

a Change the sentences from the present to the past.

1 We meet in a café. (last night)
   We met in a café last night.

2 Mateo sees his friends after work. (last night)
   _____

3 Emily loses her keys. (yesterday)
   _____

4 We don't have dinner at home. (last night)
   _____

5 They leave work at 5:30. (yesterday)
   _____

6 Alex doesn't get up early. (yesterday morning)
   _____

7 My friend feels sick. (yesterday)
   _____

8 Junko doesn't go out during the week. (last week)
   _____

9 I don't wear glasses. (yesterday)
   _____

10 Luciana can't come to my party. (last year)
   _____

b Complete the questions in the dialogue.

A Where ¹ _did you go_ last night?
B I went to that new sushi restaurant in town.
A ² _____ good?
B Yes, it was great.
A Who ³ _____ with?
B I went with my girlfriend.
A What ⁴ _____?
B I wore jeans and my new black shirt.
A What time ⁵ _____ home?
B We got home at about midnight.
A ⁶ _____ a taxi home?
B Yes. We didn't want to drive.
A Did ⁷ _____ a good time?
B Yes, we had a great time. The food was delicious!
A ⁸ _____ it expensive?
B Yes, it was.

2 VOCABULARY go, have, get

a ~~Cross out~~ the incorrect expression.

1 GO   to the beach   out   to a restaurant   ~~a bus~~
2 HAVE   lunch   a sandwich   for a walk   a sister
3 GET   dressed   a good time   up   an email
4 GO   to bed   a car   away   on vacation
5 HAVE   breakfast   a bike   short hair   18 years
6 GET   shopping   home   a newspaper   a taxi

b Complete the text with *went*, *had*, or *got*.

It was my wife's birthday last Saturday, so we ¹ _went_ away for the weekend. I booked a hotel on the Internet, and on Friday we ² _____ the train to the coast. It was late when we arrived, so we just ³ _____ a sandwich and ⁴ _____ to bed. The next day, we ⁵ _____ up early and ⁶ _____ breakfast in the hotel. It was a beautiful day, so we ⁷ _____ to the beach. We took a swim in the morning, and in the afternoon we ⁸ _____ for a walk. In the evening, we ⁹ _____ dinner in an expensive French restaurant. The food was delicious! The next day was Sunday, so we ¹⁰ _____ back home again. The weekend was very short, but we ¹¹ _____ a great time.

3 PRONUNCIATION irregular verbs, sentence stress

a Look at the pairs of irregular verbs. Do they have the same vowel sound? Write **S** (the same) or **D** (different).

1 came	had	D
2 did	feel	
3 taught	wore	
4 lost	spoke	
5 met	went	
6 knew	saw	
7 heard	left	
8 took	could	

b **iChecker** Listen and check. Then listen and repeat the irregular verbs.

c **iChecker** Listen and repeat the sentences. Copy the rhythm.

> A **What** did you **do last night**?
> B I **went** to the **movies**.
> A **Who** did you **go** with?
> B I **went** with a **friend**.
> A **Where** did you **go** after the **movies**?
> B We **went** to a **restaurant**.
> We **didn't have** an **expensive meal**.
> We **didn't get home late**.

4 LISTENING

a **iChecker** Listen to an interview about a memorable night. What did Melissa do?

b **iChecker** Listen again and answer the questions.

1 When was it?
_____.
2 Who was Melissa with?
_____.
3 Where were they?
_____.
4 When did she arrive in the city?
_____.
5 Where did they have a coffee?
_____.
6 Did they have a good time? Why (not)?
_____.
7 What did they have for dinner?
_____.
8 What time did they get home?
_____.

USEFUL WORDS AND PHRASES

Learn these words and phrases.

goal /goʊl/
moon /mun/
scarf /skɑrf/
screen /skrin/
embarrassed /ɪmˈbærəst/
memorable /ˈmɛmərəbl/
decide /dɪˈsaɪd/
take a swim /teɪk ə ˈswɪm/
know (somebody) a little /noʊ ə ˈlɪtl/

iChecker **TESTS** FILE 7

Practical English Getting lost

1 VOCABULARY directions

Complete the words.

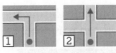
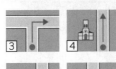

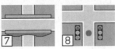

1 turn l_eft_
2 go str_____ a_____
3 turn r_____
4 go p_____ the train station
5 on the c_____
6 across f_____
7 a b_____
8 at the tr_____ l_____

2 ASKING FOR DIRECTIONS

Complete the dialogue with these words.

exactly Excuse miss near say Sorry tell way Where's

A ¹ _____Excuse_____ me, please. ² _____ the train station?
B ³ _____, I don't live here.
A Excuse me. Is the train station ⁴ _____ here?
C The train station? It's near here, but I don't know
   ⁵ _____ where. Sorry.
A Excuse me. Can you ⁶ _____ me the
   ⁷ _____ to the train station, please?
D Yes, of course. Go past the hotel. Then turn left at the
   traffic lights. It's at the end of the street.
A Sorry, could you ⁸ _____ that again, please?
D Yes. Go past the hotel. Then turn left at the traffic lights
   and it's at the end of the street. You can't
   ⁹ _____ it!
A Thank you.

3 SOCIAL ENGLISH

Complete the sentences with the words in the box.

could course meet nice Maybe there What would

1 _____What_____ a view!
2 What _____ you like to visit?
3 What is _____ to see?
4 We _____ go to the art gallery.
5 Would you like to _____ for lunch?
6 That's really _____ of you.
7 _____ another time.
8 Yes, of _____.

4 READING

a Read the information about getting around in the US.

By bus

In the US, an economical way for traveling long distances is by bus. The most important company is Greyhound, which has frequent service between big cities. Greyhound is also a convenient way for traveling to smaller cities and towns that don't have other forms of transportation like trains or airplanes. Traveling by bus is usually cheap if you buy your ticket early and travel at times of the day that are not busy.

By car

Many people travel by car in the US. It can be expensive, and there is often a lot of traffic. However, traveling by car means that you can be independent and flexible. Also, a car with three or more passengers can be cheaper than public transportation. You can go quickly from one city to the next on freeways, but small roads are often more scenic and fun. Parking in big cities can be difficult and very expensive. Some cities like Denver, Baltimore, and Philadelphia have light rail train systems. You can park outside the city in a free parking lot and then take a light rail train downtown.

By train

Trains are generally faster and more comfortable than buses for long distance travel, but they can be a lot more expensive. There is only one train company that operates train service in the US, and that is Amtrak. Passengers can get information on timetables and fares from the Amtrak website, which also has a way to buy tickets. There are three types of tickets: coach class, business class, and first class. Tickets are cheaper if you buy them early.

b Read the information again. Write T (true) or F (false).

1 Taking a bus is a slow way to travel.   _T_
2 The best time to travel by bus is at quiet times. ____
3 There isn't much traffic in the US.   ____
4 You need to pay for parking when you use
  light rail in Denver.   ____
5 You can buy tickets from Amtrak.   ____

c Match the highlighted adjectives to their meanings.

1 beautiful   _____
2 easy to do   _____
3 cheap   _____
4 easy to change something _____
5 happening often   _____

8A A murder story

1 GRAMMAR simple past: regular and irregular

a Read this police report. Complete the sentences with the simple past form of the verbs in parentheses.

POLICE REPORT

Bank robbery

We ¹ *arrived* (arrive) at the bank at 9:36 in the evening, and we ² _____ (park) our police car outside. The bank ³ _____ (be) closed and all the lights ⁴ _____ (be) off, but we ⁵ _____ (look) through the window. We ⁶ _____ (see) a person inside the bank. At first, we ⁷ _____ (not can) see who it was, but then he ⁸ _____ (open) the door and came out – it was Steven Potter. He ⁹ _____ (not run) away – he just walked slowly to his car, and then drove away. The next morning, we ¹⁰ _____ (go) to his house at 6:00 a.m. We ¹¹ _____ (find) him in bed. He ¹² _____ (not want) to speak to us, but we ¹³ _____ (take) him to the police station.

b Complete the questions with the correct form of the verbs in parentheses.

DETECTIVE   Where ¹ *were you* at about 9:30 yesterday evening? (be)

STEVEN POTTER   I was at the movies. The movie ² *started* at 9:00. (start)

D   What movie ³ _____? (see)

SP   I can't remember. It wasn't very good.

D   Hmm. Very interesting. And who ⁴ _____ to the movies with? (go)

SP   With my girlfriend.

D   ⁵ _____ the movie? (like)

SP   Yes, she thought it was very good.

D   What time ⁶ _____ the movie _____? (end)

SP   At about 10:30.

D   And what ⁷ _____ after you left the movies? (do)

SP   We went to a restaurant – La Dolce Vita on Main Street.

D   La Dolce Vita? I know it. Very good spaghetti. What time ⁸ _____ the restaurant? (leave)

SP   At about 12:00 a.m.

D   That's very late. ⁹ _____ home after that? (go)

SP   No, we went to a birthday party at Flanagan's. Then we went home.

D   How? ¹⁰ _____ a taxi? (get)

SP   No, we got a bus.

D   And what time ¹¹ _____ to bed? (go)

SP   At about 4:00 a.m. Can I go home now? I'm tired.

D   No, I'd like to ask you some more questions…

2 VOCABULARY irregular verbs

a Complete the base form and past forms of these irregular verbs with *a*, *e*, *i*, *o*, or *u*.

Base form	Past
1 beg_i_n	beg_a_n
2 c__me	c__me
3 dr__nk	dr__nk
4 dr__ve	dr__ve
5 g__ve	g__ve
6 kn__w	kn__w
7 p__t	p__t
8 s__t	s__t
9 sw__m	sw__m
10 w__ke [up]	w__ke [up]
11 w__n	w__n
12 wr__te	wr__te

b Complete the sentences with the simple past form of the verbs in the box.

buy   find   break   ~~hear~~   make   take   can   lose   meet   think

1 Last night we ___*heard*___ a noise downstairs.
2 They _____ the man's daughter was the murderer.
3 The police officer _____ the money in an old bag.
4 They _____ their friends outside the restaurant.
5 I _____ a detective story in the bookstore.
6 My wife _____ her cell phone last night.
7 The man _____ a window and went into the house.
8 Somebody _____ my laptop when I was out of the room.
9 We were worried because we _____ see a police car outside our house.
10 I was thirsty so I _____ a cup of tea.

3 PRONUNCIATION simple past verbs

a Match the verbs with the same vowel sound.

drove   could   ~~made~~   said   learned   bought   had

1 came   ___*made*___
2 left   _____
3 ran   _____
4 saw   _____
5 spoke   _____
6 took   _____
7 heard   _____

b iChecker Listen and check. Then listen and repeat.

4 LISTENING

a iChecker Listen to a radio interview with a detective. What does he like most about his job?

_____

_____

b iChecker Listen again and choose a, b, or c.

1 Jeremy Downs decided he wanted to be a detective…
   a when he was a child.
   b when he left school.
   c when he finished college.
2 His first job in the police was as…
   a a teacher.
   b a police officer.
   c a detective.
3 Jeremy took a … to make sure he was strong and healthy for the job.
   a a law test
   b a running test
   c physical fitness
4 Jeremy usually works…
   a outside.
   b in an office.
   c at the police station.
5 He sometimes feels…when he is at work.
   a bored
   b stressed
   c worried

USEFUL WORDS AND PHRASES

Learn these words and phrases.

library   /ˈlaɪbrɛri/
murder   /ˈmərdər/
nobody   /ˈnoʊbɑdi/
secretary   /ˈsɛkrətɛri/
believe   /bɪˈliv/
kill   /kɪl/
marry   /ˈmæri/
business partner   /ˈbɪznəs pɑrtnər/

8B A house with a history

1 GRAMMAR *there is / there are, some / any* + plural nouns

a Complete the dialogue with the correct form of *there is | there are* and, if necessary, *a*, *some*, or *any*.

> **A** Hello. I'm interested in the apartment for rent.
>
> **B** Oh, OK Let me tell you about it. ¹ ___*There's a*___ large living room and ² _____ small kitchen.
>
> **A** ³ _____ table in the kitchen?
>
> **B** No, ⁴ _____. But ⁵ _____ very nice dining room with a table and some chairs.
>
> **A** That's fine. What about the bedrooms? How many bedrooms ⁶ _____?
>
> **B** ⁷ _____ three bedrooms and a bathroom.
>
> **A** ⁸ _____ shower in the bathroom?
>
> **B** Yes, ⁹ _____.
>
> **A** Good. ¹⁰ _____ bookshelves in the living room?
>
> **B** No, I'm sorry. But ¹¹ _____ cupboards.
>
> **A** That's OK. I think it's perfect for us. How much is it?

b Write the sentences in the plural using *some* or *any*.

1 There's an armchair in the living room.
   ___*There are some armchairs in the living room*___.

2 Is there a rug downstairs?
   _____?

3 There's a CD on the shelf.
   _____.

4 Is there a glass in the cupboard?
   _____?

5 There isn't a light in the study.
   _____.

c Circle the correct form.

¹ **It's** / **There's** a nice apartment and ² **it isn't** / **there isn't** very expensive. ³ **There are** / **They are** two rooms, but ⁴ **there aren't** / **they aren't** very big. ⁵ **There's** / **It is** a small kitchen and a bathroom. ⁶ **There isn't** / **It isn't** a bathtub in the bathroom, but ⁷ **it's** / **there's** a new shower. The apartment is on the 10th floor, so ⁸ **there's** / **it is** a great view of the city. And ⁹ **there's** / **it's** a very large balcony with a lot of flowers. ¹⁰ **They are** / **There are** beautiful in the summer!

2 VOCABULARY the house

a Complete the crossword.

Clues across →

Clues down ↓

b Write the room.

1 You usually take off your coat in the h*all*.
2 You usually take a shower in the b_____.
3 You usually have dinner in the d_____ r_____.
4 You usually use a computer in the st_____.
5 You usually park your car in the g_____.
6 You usually make lunch in the k_____.
7 You usually watch television in the l_____ r_____.
8 You usually sleep in the b_____.
9 You usually sit outside in the y_____.

3 PRONUNCIATION /ɛr/ and /ɪr/; sentence stress

a Circle the word with a different sound.

ɛr chair	1	they're	there	dear
ɪr ear	2	cheers	stairs	near
ɛr chair	3	where	wear	we're
ɪr ear	4	here	hair	hear

b **iChecker** Listen and repeat the words.

c Underline the stressed syllable.

1 of|fice
2 mirr|or
3 cu|pboard
4 bal|co|ny
5 bath|tub
6 so|fa
7 arm|chair
8 ga|rage
9 cei|ling

d **iChecker** Listen and check. Then listen and repeat the words.

4 LISTENING

a **iChecker** Listen to Mrs. Goodings show her house to Bradley and Joanna, a couple who are interested in renting it. Check ✓ the **three** rooms Mrs. Goodings shows them.

1 bathroom ☐
2 bedroom ☐
3 dining room ☐
4 garage ☐
5 hall ☐
6 kitchen ☐
7 living room ☐
8 study ☐

b **iChecker** Listen again and write T (true) or F (false).

1 Mrs. Goodings always eats in the kitchen. _T_
2 Joanna doesn't like the living room. __
3 There isn't a washing machine in the kitchen. __
4 There's a hole in the ceiling of the kitchen. __
5 Joanna likes the windows in the living room. __
6 There isn't a TV in the living room. __
7 There are three bedrooms upstairs. __
8 Bradley forgets about the hole in the bathroom ceiling. __

USEFUL WORDS AND PHRASES

Learn these words and phrases.

advertisement /ˌædvərˈtaɪzmənt/
dishwasher /ˈdɪʃwɑʃər/
lovely /ˈlʌvli/
rent /rɛnt/
a long time ago /ə lɔŋ taɪm əˈgoʊ/
Wow! /waʊ/
How horrible! /haʊ ˈhɔrəbl/
It's perfect! /ɪts ˈpərfɪkt/

I'm not frightened of death.
I just don't want to be there when it happens.
Woody Allen, American movie director

8C A night in a haunted hotel

1 GRAMMAR *there was / there were*

a Complete the text. Use *was*, *were*, *wasn't*, or *weren't*.

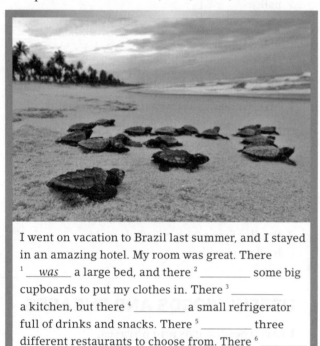

I went on vacation to Brazil last summer, and I stayed in an amazing hotel. My room was great. There
[1] __*was*__ a large bed, and there [2] _____ some big cupboards to put my clothes in. There [3] _____
a kitchen, but there [4] _____ a small refrigerator full of drinks and snacks. There [5] _____ three
different restaurants to choose from. There [6] _____
a beautiful swimming pool in the hotel, and there
[7] _____ a long beach nearby. There [8] _____
any tourists on the beach, but there [9] _____ some
baby turtles. They were really beautiful!

b Complete the dialogue with a form of *there was | there were*.

A Did you have a good vacation?
B Not really. [1] __*There was*__ a problem with my hotel.
A Oh, no. What happened?
B Well, we couldn't swim because [2] _____
a swimming pool. And [3] _____ any
restaurants near the hotel.
A [4] _____ a small refrigerator in your room?
B No, [5] _____ a small refrigerator and
[6] _____ a television. The only thing
in my room was the bed!
A Oh. [7] _____ a bathroom?
B Yes, but [8] _____ any clean towels.
Everything was very dirty.
A [9] _____ any nice people at the hotel?
B Yes, [10] _____ some great people, but they
all felt the same as me – very angry!

2 VOCABULARY prepositions: place and movement

Complete the sentences with these words.

behind	from...to	~~in~~	in front of	next to
across from	out of	over	under	up

1 There's a family __*in*__ the dining room.
2 The boy is sitting _____ the girl.
3 The woman is _____ the man.
4 There's a ghost standing _____ the woman.
5 There's a bag _____ the table.
6 A waiter is coming _____ the kitchen.
7 There's a ghost _____ the waiter.
8 The waiter is carrying the plates _____ the
kitchen _____ the tables.
9 There's a clock _____ the kitchen door.
10 A ghost is going _____ the stairs.

3 PRONUNCIATION silent letters

a ~~Cross out~~ the silent letters.

1 gh~~o~~st   3 white   5 hour   7 builder

2 cupboard   4 know   6 walk   8 wrong

b **iChecker** Listen and repeat. <u>C</u>opy the <u>rhy</u>thm.

c **iChecker** Listen and <u>underline</u> the stressed words.

1 There was a lamp on the table.
2 There wasn't a bathtub in the bathroom.
3 Was there a mirror in the bedroom?
4 There were some books on the shelf.
5 There weren't any cupboards in the kitchen.
6 Were there any plants in the study?

d **iChecker** Listen again and repeat the sentences.

4 READING

Read the text. Write T (true) or F (false).

1 Maesmawr Hall is more than 500 years old.   *F*
2 People have seen ghosts inside and outside the hotel.   —
3 The ghosts are all of people who lived in the house in the past.   —
4 Robin Drwg's ghost sometimes appears as a bull.   —
5 Paranormal investigators didn't think that Maesmawr Hall was haunted.   —

5 LISTENING

a **iChecker** Listen to four people talking about hotel rooms. Which countries did they visit?

b **iChecker** Listen again. Match the speakers to the rooms.

Speaker 1 ☐   Speaker 2 ☐   Speaker 3 ☐   Speaker 4 ☐

A The room was under the water.
B The room had mirrors on the walls and the ceiling.
C The room wasn't very comfortable.
D The room was up a tree.

USEFUL WORDS AND PHRASES

Learn these words and phrases.

ghosts /gəʊsts/
guest /gɛst/
owner /ˈəʊnər/
priest /priːst/
brave /breɪv/
frightened /ˈfraɪtnd/

haunted /ˈhɔntəd/
strange /streɪndʒ/
In the middle of the night
   /ɪn ðə mɪdl əv ðə ˈnaɪt/
remote control /rɪməʊt kənˈtrəʊl/

iChecker **TESTS** **FILE 8**

Maesmawr Hall:
A Haunted House in Wales

Maesmawr Hall is a manor house in Powys, Wales. It was built in 1535 and today is a 20-bedroom hotel and venue for weddings. It is famous because people say it is haunted.

Many guests say that they have seen ghosts. A businessman who stayed at the hotel said that when he looked out of the window, he saw hundreds of Roman soldiers marching. In fact, in Roman times there was a road that passed through the grounds of Maesmawr Hall. Other guests said they saw the ghosts of the Davies sisters who owned the hotel in the 1900s, and the ghost of an old housekeeper walking through a wall in the hall. But perhaps most frightening is the story that the ghost of an evil man named Robin Drwg haunts the woods around the hotel. Some people say that they have seen this ghost suddenly change into the shape of a bull.

Maesmawr was on a TV show about houses with ghosts called *Most Haunted*. The TV show hosts and investigators from the Mid Wales Paranormal (MWP) reported a lot of strange activity in the hall – seeing balls of light, feeling movements, and hearing unusual sounds. During the investigation, the floor in one of the upstairs rooms moved. The hotel's current owner, Nigel Humphryson, says he often hears voices and banging noises that he cannot explain.

So if you're interested in ghosts, why not stay here? But don't go outside at night unless you're feeling really brave!

To eat well in England, have breakfast
three times a day.
W. Somerset Maugham, British writer

9A What I ate yesterday

1 GRAMMAR countable / uncountable nouns; *a / an*, *some / any*

a What did Sarah and Martin buy when they went shopping yesterday? Write *a*, *an*, or *some* in the blanks.

1 _*some*_____ sausages   6 _____ orange
2 _____ lettuce   7 _____ pineapple
3 _____ eggs   8 _____ potato chips
4 _____ carrots   9 _____ cookies
5 _____ jam   10 _____ milk

b Write the sentences in the affirmative ⊞ or negative ⊟ form.

1 There's some cheese in the refrigerator.
⊟ There _isn't any cheese in the refrigerator_____.

2 There are some strawberries in our garden.
⊟ There _____.

3 I didn't have an egg for breakfast.
⊞ I _____.

4 There isn't any sugar in my tea.
⊞ There _____.

5 I didn't eat any snacks yesterday.
⊞ I _____.

6 There weren't any sandwiches in the kitchen.
⊞ There _____.

7 I bought a pineapple at the supermarket.
⊟ I _____.

8 There was some bread in the cupboard.
⊟ There _____.

c Complete the dialogue with *a*, *an*, *some*, or *any*.

A What do we need to buy for our dinner party? Let's make a list.
B Well, I want to make ¹ _*a*_ lasagne, so we need ² _____ pasta and ³ _____ meat.
A Pasta...and meat. What about tomatoes? Are there ⁴ _____ tomatoes in the refrigerator?
B Let's look. There's ⁵ _____ onion, but there aren't ⁶ _____ tomatoes. Put those on the list, too.
A OK...tomatoes. Is there ⁷ _____ cheese?
B Yes, there's ⁸ _____ mozzarella cheese, so that's perfect.
A Let's have ⁹ _____ salad with the lasagna.
B OK. Then we need to buy ¹⁰ _____ lettuce.
A What about dessert? Is there ¹¹ _____ fruit?
B No, there isn't. Let's get ¹² _____ strawberries.

2 VOCABULARY food

a Complete the crossword.

Clues across →

Clues down ↓

b Write the words in the correct column.

apples bananas candy carrots chocolate cookies
mushrooms onions oranges peas pineapple
potatoes potato chips sandwiches strawberries

Vegetables	Snacks	Fruit
_____	_____	*apples*
_____	_____	_____
_____	_____	_____
_____	_____	_____
_____	_____	_____

3 PRONUNCIATION the letters ea

a (Circle) the word with a different sound.

🌳 tree (i)	1	meat breakfast **tea**
🥚 egg (ɛ)	2	bread healthy ice cream
🚂 train (eɪ)	3	eat great steak

b **iChecker** Listen and check. Then listen and repeat the words.

4 READING

a Read the article and match the headings to the paragraphs.

coconut water   popsicles   roast camel

b Read the article again. Write T (true) or F (false).

1 The Bedouin people eat roast camel on special occasions. *T*

2 There are seven ingredients in the Bedouin meal. ___

3 Frank Epperson's drink froze because the weather was cold. ___

4 He sold his first ice pop when he was 29 years old. ___

5 According to the article, you can find coconut water in all coconuts. ___

6 Coconut water has a lot of sugar. ___

c Guess the meaning of the highlighted words. Check in your dictionary.

5 LISTENING

a **iChecker** Listen to four speakers talking about their favorite meal. Complete the meals.

Speaker 1   roast _____
Speaker 2   _____ tikka masala
Speaker 3   hot dog and _____
Speaker 4   sweet and sour tofu and _____

b **iChecker** Listen again. Match the speakers to the sentences.

Speaker 1 ☐   A I often eat it outside.
Speaker 2 ☐   B I always order rice with it.
Speaker 3 ☐   C I have it at a local restaurant.
Speaker 4 ☐   D I eat it when I visit my parents.

USEFUL WORDS AND PHRASES

Learn these words and phrases.

cream /krim/
dishes /ˈdɪʃɪz/
ingredients /ɪnˈɡridiənts/
popcorn /ˈpɑpkɔrn/
sauce /sɔs/
sweet corn /ˈswit kɔrn/
(food) to go /ˈtoʊ ɡoʊ/
delicious /dɪˈlɪʃəs/
vegetarian /vɛdʒəˈtɛriən/

Three interesting food facts

1 _____

The Bedouin people, who live in the deserts of Africa, sometimes prepare a very big meal to celebrate weddings. The cook uses some eggs, some fish, some chickens, a sheep, and a camel to prepare it. He stuffs the fish with the eggs, the chickens with the fish, the sheep with the chickens, and the camel with the sheep. Then he cooks all the ingredients together in an enormous oven in the ground.

2 _____

It was an 11-year-old American boy who invented these. In 1905, the boy, Frank Epperson, wanted to make a drink. He put some soda powder in a cup of water and used a stick to mix it. Then he forgot about the drink and left it outside. That night it was very cold, so the mixture froze. Eighteen years later, he made some more of the frozen mixture and sold his first one at an amusement park. The British call them "ice pops."

3 _____

You can find this liquid in young fruit that is still green. People drank it in South-East Asia, Africa, and the Caribbean before it became popular as a health drink. Today, athletes drink it after playing sports. It is very good for you as it is low in fats and sugars. Doctors sometimes use it in an emergency because it is similar to human plasma.

Human beings are 70% water.
With some people, the rest is collagen.

Martin Mull, American actor and writer

9B White gold

1 GRAMMAR quantifiers: *how much / how many, a lot of,* etc.

a Complete the questions. Then complete the sentences.

How much salt do you put on your food?

Not much.

_____ _____ sugar do you put in your tea?

A lot.

_____ _____ cookies do you eat?

Not many.

1 He *doesn't put much salt on his food*.

2 He _____.

3 She _____.

_____ _____ candy do you buy?

A lot.

_____ _____ exercise do you do?

Not much.

_____ _____ cups of coffee do you drink?

None.

4 He _____.

5 He _____.

6 She _____.

b Read the information and write questions.

FOOD FACTS

There is .81 ounces of sugar in an orange.

There are about 125 calories in a banana.

There are about 18 oranges in a carton of orange juice.

There is .04 ounces of salt in a bowl of cereal.

There are twelve eggs in a carton.

There are 16 ounces of jam in a jar.

1 _How much sugar is there in an orange_ ?
Answer: .81 ounces.

2 _____ ?
Answer: About 125.

3 _____ ?
Answer: About 18.

4 _____ ?
Answer: .04 ounces.

5 _____ ?
Answer: twelve.

6 _____ ?
Answer: 16 ounces.

2 VOCABULARY food containers

a Unscramble the words to make food containers.

1 rja   _jar_
2 bxo   _____
3 rncoat   _____
4 gab   _____
5 cpeagka   _____
6 nca   _____
7 totble   _____

b Complete the sentences with a container from **a**.

1 She was thirsty, so she bought a ___can___ of soda.
2 Do you need the scissors to open the _____ of juice?
3 He took the _____ of strawberry jam out of the cupboard.
4 There is a large _____ of potato chips on the table.
5 We always take a _____ of water when we go for a walk.
6 Ken feels sick because he ate a big _____ of cookies.
7 I gave her a _____ of chocolates to say thank you.

3 PRONUNCIATION /ʃ/ and /s/

a Circle the word with a different sound.

snake	1	**s**ugar	**s**alad	**c**ereal
shower	2	**s**ure	fre**sh**	**s**alt
snake	3	ri**c**e	**sh**opping	**sc**ience
shower	4	**sh**ort	informa**ti**on	**c**enter

b iChecker Listen and check. Then listen and repeat the words.

c iChecker Listen and repeat the sentences.

1 She saw Susan standing outside the study.
2 Shawn said sorry for singing in the shower.
3 Steve puts six spoons of sugar on his cereal.
4 Sylvia spends Saturdays in the shopping center.

4 LISTENING

a iChecker Listen to the radio program about food groups. Complete the examples of the groups.

1 carbohydrates: bread, pasta, _____, potatoes
2 fruits and vegetables: apples, oranges, _____, carrots
3 protein: meat, _____
4 milk and dairy: _____, yogurt
5 fats and sugars: cake, _____, candy, chips

b iChecker Listen again. Fill in the blanks with one word.

1 Carbohydrates give us _____.
2 Fruits and vegetables contain important _____.
3 Protein helps our bodies to _____ and repair.
4 Milk and dairy are important for our bones and _____.
5 You should eat fats and sugars _____ or _____ a week.

USEFUL WORDS AND PHRASES

Learn these words and phrases.

gold /goʊld/
spoon /spun/
vitamins /ˈvaɪtəmənz/
fresh /frɛʃ/
spoonful /ˈspunfʊl/
instead of /ɪnˈstɛd əv/

9C Quiz night

1 GRAMMAR comparative adjectives

a Write the comparative forms of these adjectives in the correct circle.

~~bad~~ beautiful cheap dry sad difficult dirty cold far wet high hungry comfortable thin good

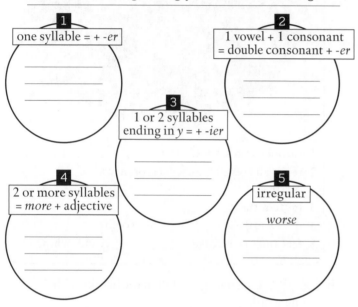

1 one syllable = + *-er*

2 1 vowel + 1 consonant = double consonant + *-er*

3 1 or 2 syllables ending in *y* = + *-ier*

4 2 or more syllables = *more* + adjective

5 irregular

worse

b Write sentences using the opposite adjective.

1 A bike is slower than a car.
A car ___is faster than a bike___ .

2 Lions are smaller than tigers.
Tigers _____ .

3 Brazil is wetter than Argentina.
Argentina _____ .

4 January is longer than February.
February _____ .

5 A laptop is more expensive than an iPod.
An iPod _____ .

6 Fridays are better than Mondays.
Mondays _____ .

7 A stove is hotter than a refrigerator.
A refrigerator _____ .

8 Spanish is easier than English.
English _____ .

2 VOCABULARY high numbers

a **iChecker** Listen and circle the correct numbers.

1	104	304
2	586	596
3	2,670	2,660
4	8,905	9,905
5	11,750	12,750
6	543, 830	553,830
7	1,315,000	1,350,000
8	25,460,000	35,460,000

b **iChecker** Listen and write the numbers in words.

1 125 _____

2 895 _____

3 4,500 _____

4 12,470 _____

5 33,930 _____

6 575,600 _____

7 6,250,000 _____

8 34,800,265 _____

3 PRONUNCIATION /ər/, sentence stress

a Write the words in the chart.

~~better~~ bigger cheaper colder dirtier drier easier healthier higher slower thinner worse

tree	fish	bird	egg	phone	bike
			better		

b **iChecker** Listen and repeat.

c (iChecker) Listen and <u>underline</u> the stressed words.

1 A pencil is cheaper than a pen.
2 China is bigger than Japan.
3 The kitchen is dirtier than the living room.
4 An apple is healthier than a cookie.
5 Canada is colder than Mexico.
6 Everest is higher than Kilimanjaro.

d (iChecker) Listen again and repeat the sentences. <u>Copy</u> the <u>rhythm</u>.

4 READING

a Read the sentences. Do you think they are T (true) or F (false)? Then read the article and check.

1 There are fewer car accidents on Tax Day. __
2 Elephants remember more than other animals. __
3 South America is bigger than North America. __
4 Margarine is healthier than butter. __

b Guess the meaning of the highlighted words. Check the meaning and pronunciation in your dictionary.

5 LISTENING

(iChecker) Listen to a conversation between a couple talking about two cities with the same name. Write T (true) or F (false).

1 More people live in Birmingham, UK than Birmingham, US. _T_
2 Birmingham, US is bigger than Birmingham, UK. __
3 Birmingham, US is greener than Birmingham, UK. __
4 Birmingham, US is older than Birmingham, UK. __
5 Birmingham, US is wetter than Birmingham, UK. __
6 Birmingham, US is hotter than Birmingham, UK. __

USEFUL WORDS AND PHRASES

Learn these words and phrases.

contestants /kənˈtɛstənts/
population /pɑpyəˈleɪʃn/
prize /praɪz/
approximately /əˈprɑksəmətli/
win a competition /wɪn ə kɑmpəˈtɪʃn/

(iChecker) (TESTS) FILE 9

Modern *myths*

1 Elephants have brains that are bigger than any other land mammal. The expression "an elephant never forgets" suggests that the bigger an animal's brain is, the better that animal can remember things. Animal researchers discovered that this is actually true for elephants! These animals can remember details about areas of land as big as 1,200 square miles!

2 There are 12 countries in South America including Argentina and Brazil. It has an area of 6,888,062 square miles and its population is over 371,090,000. North America includes Canada and the US, but it also contains the countries of Central America. It covers an area of about 95,401,198 square miles, and its population is almost 529 million. This makes it bigger than South America.

3 When the *American Medical Association* studied the number of people injured in traffic accidents in the US, they got a surprise. They discovered that there were more dangerous car accidents on Tax Day. Tax Day is every year around April 15. People in the US are busy around this time!

4 Experts have different opinions about margarine and butter, and there is a big argument about which one is better for you. The truth is that margarine today is better than it was in the past because producers use a different type of vegetable oil. Butter still contains a lot of animal fat. Margarine today contains less fat which makes it healthier than butter.

1 VOCABULARY AND READING

a Look at the menu and answer the questions.

1 Which is the best appetizer for somebody on a diet?
2 What main course can a vegetarian have?
3 Can you have fruit for dessert?
4 How many types of coffee are there?
5 Do children pay the same as adults?

Taste of Heaven Restaurant
MENU

Appetizers

Chicken soup	$6.50
Shrimp cocktail	$9.25
Grilled vegetables with low-fat cheese (V)	$6.75

Salads

Tossed salad (V)	$5.50
Seafood salad	$7.25

Main courses

Roast beef served with roast potatoes and vegetables	$19.25
Mushroom risotto with Parmesan cheese (V)	$11.50
Grilled salmon served with French fries and peas	$16.75

Desserts

Fresh fruit salad	$6.95
Chocolate brownie with cream	$8.50
New York cheesecake	$8.25

Beverages

Iced tea	$2.75
Soda	$2.75
Coffee (espresso or latte)	$2.25

Today's specials

$19.95 (see the board for the daily specials)

25% discount on children's portions
(V) Suitable for vegetarians

b Underline the words or phrases you don't know. Use your dictionary to look up their meaning and pronunciation.

2 ORDERING A MEAL

Complete the dialogue with <u>one</u> word in each blank.

A Good evening. Do you have a [1] _reservation_ ?
B Yes, a [2] _____ for two. My name's Regina Morgan.
A Come this [3] _____ , please.
A Are you ready to [4] _____ ?
B Yes. The grilled vegetables and the mushroom risotto, please.
C [5] _____ like the shrimp cocktail and then the roast beef, please.
A What would you [6] _____ to drink?
C [7] _____ water for me.
B A bottle of mineral water, please.
A [8] _____ or sparkling?
B Is sparkling OK?
C Yes, sparkling.
A Thank you, madam.
B Thank you.

3 SOCIAL ENGLISH

Match the sentences 1–6 to the correct responses a–f.

1 What do you do on your birthday? `c`
2 Would you like a dessert? ☐
3 A decaf espresso. ☐
4 Can I use your phone? ☐
5 Good news? ☐
6 Could we have the bill, please? ☐

a Not for me, thanks.
b Yes. I got the job!
c ~~Nothing special.~~
d Yes, of course, sir.
e The same for me, please.
f Yes, go ahead.

As soon as there is life there is danger.
Ralph Waldo Emerson, American writer

10A The most dangerous road...

1 GRAMMAR superlative adjectives

a Complete the chart.

Adjective	Comparative	Superlative
1 cold	*colder*	*the coldest*
2 high		
3 expensive		
4 dry		
5 dangerous		
6 hot		
7 beautiful		
8 interesting		
9 good		
10 bad		

b Write the questions.

1 What / small continent / world
What's the smallest continent in the world ?
2 What / big ocean / world
_______________?
3 What / large country / world
_______________?
4 What / populated city / world
_______________?
5 What / wet place / world
_______________?
6 What / dry desert / world
_______________?
7 What / common native language / world
_______________?
8 What / cold place / world
_______________?

c Circle the correct answer to the questions in **b**.

1 a (Australia)
b Europe
c South America

2 a The Atlantic
b The Pacific
c The Indian Ocean

3 a Canada
b China
c Russia

4 a Mumbai
b Shanghai
c Buenos Aires

5 a India
b Ireland
c Brazil

6 a The Sahara Desert (Africa)
b The Painted Desert (The US)
c The Atacama Desert (South America)

7 a Mandarin Chinese
b English
c Hindi

8 a The Arctic
b Alaska
c The Antarctic

2 VOCABULARY places and buildings

a Complete the sentences with a word in each box.

art department parking police post ~~shopping~~ town train

gallery hall lot ~~mall~~ office station station store

1 Where can you visit different stores?
At a *shopping mall* .
2 Where can you see paintings?
In an _______ _______.
3 Where can you get a train from?
From a _______ _______.
4 Where can you buy a stamp?
At a _______ _______.
5 Where can you talk to a police officer?
At a _______ _______.
6 Where can you buy clothes for all the family?
At a _______ _______.
7 Where can you leave your car?
At a _______ _______.
8 Where can you speak to a local politician?
In the _______ _______.

b Complete the puzzle. Can you find the hidden word?

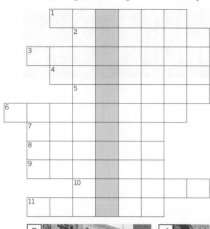

3 PRONUNCIATION consonant groups

iChecker Listen and repeat the sentences.

1 It's the cheapest place to live.
2 It's the highest mountain in the world.
3 He's the healthiest person in the family.
4 It's the prettiest town in the country.
5 It's the most difficult language to learn.
6 It's the most polluted city in the area.
7 They're the most attractive couple I know.
8 She's the most intelligent person in the class.

4 LISTENING

a **iChecker** Listen to a radio interview with a travel writer.
What is his book called? _____

b **iChecker** Listen again. Complete the sentences.

1 Uluru is the _____ rock in the world.
2 It's _____ feet long.
3 The world's highest waterfall is in _____.
4 The tallest building in the world is _____ feet high.
5 The world's oldest city began in _____ BC.
6 The world's longest train track goes from _____
   to Vladivostok.
7 The shortest runway in the world is _____ feet long.

5 READING

a Read the text and write T (true) or F (false).

1 Ulm Münster is the world's biggest church. ___
2 You can sometimes see the mountains from the top of the church. ___
3 Ulm Münster was the city's first church. ___
4 Construction of the church took over 500 years. ___
5 The church opens every day at 8 o'clock. ___
6 It's very expensive to visit Ulm Münster. ___

b Guess the meaning of the highlighted words. Check in your dictionary.

THE SKY'S THE LIMIT

Ulm Münster in Germany is the tallest church in the world. The tallest part of the church is the steeple, which is 528 feet high and contains 768 steps. From the top of the church there is a view of the city, and on a clear day you can see the Alps.

Before the Münster was built, Ulm already had a church outside the city walls. However, the inhabitants of the city decided that they wanted a new church in the town center, and they agreed to pay for the building.

Construction of the church began in 1377, but the building wasn't completed until May 31, 1890. At first, the work was difficult because the heaviest parts fell down and the builders had to repair them. Then construction stopped from 1543 to 1817 for political reasons.

Today, tourists can visit the church every day of the year. In the winter, the church is open from 9 a.m. to 4:45 p.m. and the church is open in the summer months from 8 a.m. to 7:45 p.m. Admission to the church is free, but the price of climbing the steeple is €3 for adults and €2 for children.

USEFUL WORDS AND PHRASES

Learn these words and phrases.

accidents /ˈæksədənts/
fun /fʌn/
region /ˈriːdʒən/
almost /ˈɔːlmoʊst/
popular /ˈpɑpyələr/
wide (*opposite* narrow) /waɪd/
below (*opposite* above) /bɪˈloʊ/

10B CouchSurf around the world!

1 GRAMMAR *be going to* (plans), future time expressions

a Order the words to make sentences.

1 are / there / you / get / to / How / going
   <u>How are you going to get there</u>?

2 to / isn't / He / a / going / stay / in / hotel
   _____.

3 show / to / They're / city / going / the / me
   _____.

4 good / going / time / have / We're / to / a
   _____.

5 is / home / to / she / going / When / go
   _____?

6 not / sights / going / I'm / see / the / to
   _____.

b Complete the sentences. Use the correct form of *going to*.

1 <u>Are they going to leave</u> by train? (they / leave)
2 We _____ our friends the city. (show)
3 They _____ nice meals in expensive restaurants. (have)
4 _____ with a friend? (you / stay)
5 They _____ the museum. (not visit)
6 _____ the sights? (they / see)
7 He _____ a lot of people. (meet)
8 She _____ on vacation this year. (not go)

c Complete the dialogue. Use the correct form of *going to*.

A So, where ¹ <u>are you going to go</u> (go) on vacation?
B I ² _____ (travel) around the US for a few weeks.
A Really? Where ³ _____ (stay)?
B Well, this year I ⁴ _____ (not/sleep) in hotels. Instead, I'm going to CouchSurf.
A CouchSurf? What a great idea! ⁵ _____ (travel) alone?
B Yes, I am. My best friend ⁶ _____ (drive) to San Diego with some friends. They ⁷ _____ (spend) all day on the beach, and they ⁸ _____ (dance) all night. I don't like that kind of vacation. I ⁹ _____ (meet) a lot of new people and see a lot of new places.
A Which states ¹⁰ _____? (visit)
B Virginia first, and then North Carolina, South Carolina, and Georgia. My CouchSurfing hosts ¹¹ _____ (show) me the sights. I ¹² _____ (have) a great time!

2 VOCABULARY vacations

a Write the expressions in the correct column.

~~back home~~   by train   a good time   on vacation
the sights   in a hotel   nice meals
somebody around your town   with a friend

GO	*back home*
HAVE	
SEE	
SHOW	
STAY	

b Complete the text with the verbs from **a**.

Maria is really happy because she's going to ¹ <u>go</u> on vacation tomorrow. She's going to ² _____ with her cousins in Buenos Aires. They're going to ³ _____ her around the city, and she's going to ⁴ _____ all the sights. They're going to ⁵ _____ a lot of nice meals together. She's going to ⁶ _____ by plane, and she's going to ⁷ _____ in Buenos Aires for a week. The second week, Maria and her cousins are going to travel to the coast. They're going to ⁸ _____ in a hotel, and they're going to ⁹ _____ a great time. Maria's going to ¹⁰ _____ back to Buenos Aires before she goes home.

3 PRONUNCIATION sentence stress

a (iChecker) Listen and underline the stressed words.

1 How are you going to get there?
2 Where are you going to stay?
3 We're going to stay for a week.
4 I'm going to see the sights.
5 We aren't going to go by car.
6 I'm not going to stay in a hotel.

b (iChecker) Listen again and repeat the sentences.
   Copy the rhythm.

4 LISTENING

a (iChecker) Listen to four speakers talking about
   their first experience CouchSurfing. How many
   people did not enjoy the experience? _____

b (iChecker) Listen again and match the speakers
   to the sentences A–D.

Speaker 1 ☐   Speaker 3 ☐
Speaker 2 ☐   Speaker 4 ☐

A CouchSurfing gave me the chance to make friends.
B CouchSurfing helped me with my work.
C My host was also my tour guide to the city.
D My second experience CouchSurfing was better
   than the first.

5 READING

a Read the text. Answer the questions with **A** (Angela),
   J (Jay), **S** (Sofia), or **T** (Tomo).

1 Which person made new friends while traveling? ☐
2 Who spent very little on accomodations? ☐
3 Who used his or her InterRail pass on another
   form of transportation? ☐
4 Who was traveling abroad for the first time? ☐
5 Which person found it easy to make new plans
   while traveling? ☐

USEFUL WORDS AND PHRASES

Learn these words and phrases.

couch /kaʊtʃ/
roommate /'rʊmmeɪt/
a host /ə 'hoʊst/
create a profile /kri'eɪt ə 'proʊfaɪl/
recommend (things to do) /rɛkə'mɛnd/
Have a good trip! /hæv ə gʊd 'trɪp/
It's free. /ɪts 'fri/
Things didn't work out. /θɪŋz 'dɪdnt wɜrk aʊt/

Traveling by InterRail

Since 1972, backpackers have enjoyed the freedom to
explore 30 European countries thanks to the InterRail pass.
Here, InterRail travelers say why they love InterRail so much.

Angela Bowman, (23, the US)

Route
Amsterdam – Hamburg – Berlin – Warsaw – Krakow – Prague – Vienna – Budapest – Zagreb – Split – Mostar – Sarajevo – Belgrade

I love InterRail because you can go where you want, when
you want! When we started our trip, we had an idea of
where we wanted to go, but as we traveled, we got new ideas.
Changing our plans was easy – you can stay an extra night
or two if you like a place, and if you don't like it, you can go
somewhere else. The InterRail pass gives you real freedom.

Jay Honahan (26, Canada)

Route
Amsterdam – Bonn – Stuttgart – Salzburg – Ljubljana – Split – Pescara – Bari – Corfu – Igoumenitsa – Patras – Athens

One of the best things about InterRail is that you get cheaper,
or even free travel on ferries as well as trains. I traveled to Split
in Croatia and then took the ferry to Pescara in Italy. Then I
traveled by InterRail to the south of Italy and then took the
ferry to the Greek island of Corfu. It was fantastic! You also get
discounts on hotels, tourist attractions, and a lot more.

Sofia Valenzuela (26, Mexico)

Route
Paris – Versailles – Épernay – Blois – Angers – Lyons – Chamonix – Nice – Monaco – Ventimiglia – Pisa – Florence – Perugia – Assisi – Rome – Naples

In six weeks, I met so many new, interesting people and
made friends from all over the world. It's a cheap way to
travel too, especially if you take the night trains – I saved
a lot of money on accomodations this way. I really want to
go InterRailing again!

Tomo Nagasaki (21, Japan)

Route
Innsbruck – Venice – Sienna – Lucca – Pisa – Florence – Cannes – Monaco – Nice – Figueras – Rosas – Barcelona – Paris – Antwerp

This was the first time I'd left Japan, and I loved it. InterRail
is safe and easy for first-time travelers. I got an InterRail
Global Pass so I could take as many trains as I wanted. I
saw many amazing places, and learned a lot about Europe's
culture and history. I visited over 15 cities in less than a
month. I'm definitely going to do it again next year!

10C What's going to happen?

1 GRAMMAR *be going to* (predictions)

a Look at the pictures. Write sentences using these verbs and *be going to*.

buy   change   ~~eat~~   have   listen   lose   read   take

1 *They're going to eat*   a pizza.
2 _____ some money.
3 _____ a newspaper.
4 _____ a coffee.
5 _____ to music.
6 _____ a book.
7 _____ a photo.
8 _____ his passport.

b Write a letter in the box: **A** = plan, **B** = prediction.

1 I'm going to buy some stamps.   [A]
2 It's going to be cold tomorrow.   ☐
3 Jim's going to study tonight.   ☐
4 Our team is going to lose this game.   ☐
5 There's going to be a storm later.   ☐
6 I think that restaurant's going to close.   ☐
7 They're going to buy a new TV.   ☐
8 I'm going to book a flight online.   ☐

2 VOCABULARY verb phrases

Complete the phrases with verbs from the box.

~~be~~   become   fall   get (x3)   ~~have~~   meet   move   travel

1 *be*   lucky
2 _____ somebody new
3 _____ to a different country
4 _____ married
5 _____ a lot of money
6 _____ in love
7 _____ famous
8 _____ a new job
9 *have*   a surprise
10 _____ to a new house

3 PRONUNCIATION the letters *oo*

a Look at the pairs of words. Check ✓ the pairs with the same sound and put an ✗ on the pairs that are different.

1 choose	school	✓
2 book	soon	✗
3 food	moon	
4 good	cook	
5 took	spoon	
6 look	too	

b (iChecker) Listen and check. Then listen and repeat.

4 READING

a Read the text. Match the headings to the paragraphs.

1 Give me your hand   3 How do you like your tea?
2 Let's play cards   4 What's inside the ball?

b Read the text again and write T (true) or F (false).

1 The easiest way to read tarot cards is to use four cards. ___
2 An image of a nurse means bad health. ___
3 A strong heart line means you're going to find love. ___
4 A shape of a bird means bad luck. ___

c Guess the meaning of the highlighted words. Check in your dictionary.

5 LISTENING

a (iChecker) Listen to Pete and Amy's conversation about the psychic Uri Geller. Was his trick with the spoons real?

b (iChecker) Listen again and write T (true) or F (false).

1 A lot of people watched Uri Geller in the past. ___
2 Pete and Amy see a video of the trick. ___
3 Amy doesn't believe the trick at first. ___
4 Uri doesn't use a normal spoon. ___
5 Uri doesn't speak during the trick. ___
6 Today, Uri doesn't appear in public. ___

The name behind *the method*

A _____

In tasseography, *the fortune-teller uses tea leaves to predict the future. You drink a cup of tea and leave a small amount in the bottom of the cup. Then you move the tea around the cup three times, cover it with a saucer, and turn it upside down. The fortune-teller looks at the shape the tea leaves make. For example, a bird means that you're going to have good news.*

B _____

In crystallomancy, *the fortune-teller uses a glass ball. She places the ball on the table between you and her, and looks into it for a long period of time. At first, the ball looks dull and cloudy, but then it clears and images start to appear. The fortune-teller uses these pictures to predict your future. For example, a nurse means that you're going to be sick.*

C _____

In tarot reading, *the fortune-teller uses a special pack of tarot cards to predict the future. There are 78 cards in the pack, and there are different ways of using them. The quickest is to lay three cards on the table from left to right. The cards represent the past, the present, and the future. The fortune-teller turns over the cards and says what they mean. For example, the sun means that you're going to become famous.*

D _____

Chiromancy is also called palmistry *and it's when the fortune-teller studies the lines on the palm of your hand to predict your future. There are four major lines on the hand: the life line, the head line, the heart line, and the health line. For example, a strong heart line means that you're going to find the right partner and be happy in your life.*

USEFUL WORDS AND PHRASES

Learn these words and phrases.

soon /suːn/
be lucky /bi ˈlʌki/
Come in! /kʌm ɪn/
get married /gɛt ˈmærid/
move to another country /muːv tu əˈnʌðər ˈkʌntri/

(iChecker) (TESTS) FILE 10

You can fall in love at first sight with a place as with a person.

Alec Waugh, British writer

11A First impressions

1 GRAMMAR adverbs (manners and modifiers)

a Complete the sentences with an adverb.

1 The French cook perfect meals.
   They cook ___perfectly___ .
2 The Americans are careful drivers.
   They drive _____ .
3 The British are very polite.
   They speak very _____ .
4 The Brazilians are good at soccer.
   They play soccer _____ .
5 The Japanese are very hard workers.
   They work very _____ .
6 The Canadians eat healthy food.
   They eat _____ .
7 The Argentinians are beautiful dancers.
   They dance _____ .

b Circle the correct word.

1 My brother dresses **casual** / **casually**.
2 Shoji cooks **real** / **really** well.
3 It's **easy** / **easily** to ride a bike.
4 They walked **quick** / **quickly** to the train station.
5 He's very **quiet** / **quietly**. He never says anything!
6 Elena's pizzas are **incredible** / **incredibly**.
7 My French is very **bad** / **badly**.
8 Can you speak more **slow** / **slowly**?
9 Mark speaks English **good** / **well**.
10 She eats **unhealthily** / **unhealthy**.
11 They have **real** / **really** stressful jobs.

2 VOCABULARY common adverbs

Make adverbs from the adjectives and complete the sentences.

careful	good	easy	hard	healthy	incredible	perfect	quiet

In the ideal city...
1 ...car drivers drive ___carefully___ .
2 ...workers work _____ .
3 ...families eat _____ .
4 ...people speak foreign languages _____ .
5 ...you can travel around _____ .
6 ...people talk _____ .
7 ...everybody treats tourists _____ .
8 ...everything is _____ cheap.

3 PRONUNCIATION word stress

a Underline the stressed syllable in the adverbs. Which **three** adverbs are not stressed on the first syllable?

_____ , _____ , _____

1 beau|ti|ful|ly   4 dan|ge|rous|ly   7 per|fect|ly
2 care|ful|ly   5 fa|shio|na|bly   8 po|lite|ly
3 ca|su|al|ly   6 in|cre|di|bly   9 un|heal|thi|ly

b **iChecker** Listen and check. Then listen and repeat the adverbs.

4 READING

a Read the text. Match the headings A-D to the paragraphs.

   A The Mexican way of life
   B Feeling at home abroad
   C My first impressions
   D Not what I expected

First impressions of Mexico City

Christina Hornick, from the US, came to Mexico for the first time three years ago. She now lives in Mexico City where she is a teacher.

1 _____

You always remember your first impressions of a new country. When I first came to Mexico City, I didn't know much about Mexico at all. I didn't know anything about the culture. I didn't think the food was very different from American food, and I expected the weather to be similar to North Carolina in the US—maybe even warmer! But when I got there, I discovered how wrong I was.

2 _____

It was summer, and it was warm, but not hot. In fact, the temperature was about 70 degrees Fahrenheit. My first impression was that Mexico City was more beautiful than I expected. I spent a lot of time looking at the incredible architecture. The city was so colorful and had a wonderful atmosphere. I saw pink, yellow, and red houses. The trees were colorful too with pink and purple flowers.

3 _____

Mexican people are very friendly. A lot of Mexicans can speak a little English, and some speak it very well. I speak Spanish pretty well, but when I make a mistake, my Mexican friends don't mind. Mexican people are very hospitable and they love to socialize —get together, eat, dance, and play music. At parties, there is often a lot of delicious, homemade food to eat. And there is often very loud music which makes it hard to hear people!

4 _____

Mexico is a great place to live. It has everything—friendly people, great public transportation, and delicious food. In Mexico City, the summers are warm, and the winters are cool. It's great weather for long walks in the nearby canyons. Mexico has mountains, lakes, beaches, and rivers. It has many beautiful cities and a fascinating culture. I still love the US, but Mexico feels like home now.

b Complete the sentences with words in the box.

atmosphere	culture	socializing	fascinating
hospitality	architecture	expect	

1 Before she went to Mexico City, Christina didn't know much about Mexican _____.
2 She didn't _____ the city to be so beautiful.
3 She was very impressed by the _____ in Mexico City.
4 She liked the colors and the wonderful _____ of the city.
5 The _____ of the Mexican people is warm and welcoming.
6 Mexican people like _____ with their friends and family.
7 Christina finds the Mexican culture _____ .

c Guess the meaning of the highlighted words. Check with your dictionary.

5 LISTENING

iChecker Listen to two people talking about where they live. Answer the questions.

Speaker 1   Toronto, Canada

1 Where don't people usually go on the weekends?
2 How do people normally dress during the week?
3 Why is Toronto's nickname "Hollywood North?"

Speaker 2   Reykjavik, Iceland

4 When do people go to swimming pools and hot tubs?
5 What are there very few of in the Icelandic countryside?
6 How many people are there…?
   in Reykjavik
   in the second-biggest city
7 What kind of things do Icelandic people make?

USEFUL WORDS AND PHRASES

Learn these words and phrases.

a foreigner /ˈfɔrənər/
myth /mɪθ/
subtitles /ˈsʌbtaɪtlz/
incredible /ɪnˈkrɛdəbl/
incredibly /ɪnˈkrɛdəbli/
dress (well) /ˈdrɛs/
a strong accent /ə strɔŋ ˈæksɛnt/
first impressions /fərst ɪmˈprɛʃnz/
get dark /gɛt ˈdɑrk/
in general /ɪn ˈdʒɛnərəl/
lock (your) doors /lɑk ˈdɔrz/

11B What do you want to do?

1 GRAMMAR verb + infinitive

a Complete the sentences with *to* and a verb in the box.

| become cook download go ride spend |
| stop visit |

1 I'd like _to go_ on a safari.
2 My brother's learning _____ a motorcycle.
3 Do you need _____ less time on your computer?
4 She wants _____ biting her nails.
5 Would you like _____ New York City?
6 We know all their songs, so we don't need _____ the lyrics.
7 I'm leaving home next month so I need to learn _____ a meal.
8 Do you want _____ a singer?

b Write sentences or questions with *would like*. Use contractions.

1 he / have very long hair ⊟
   He wouldn't like to have very long hair .
2 you / climb a mountain ⍰
   _____
   _____ ?
3 we / get up earlier ⊞
   _____
   _____ .
4 I / learn to fly a plane ⊞
   _____
   _____ .
5 she / make a short movie ⊟
   _____
   _____ .
6 they / get married ⍰
   _____
   _____ ?

2 VOCABULARY verbs that take the infinitive

Match the sentences 1–8 with the sentences a–h.

1 I'm taking some lessons. 　⍰*f*
2 Our washing machine is broken. 　☐
3 I have a lot of dresses. 　☐
4 I'm playing tennis tomorrow. 　☐
5 That girl is Brazilian so I can't speak to her. 　☐
6 We are looking at hotels in Miami, Florida. 　☐
7 I don't have time to do my homework now. 　☐
8 I love Carrie Underwood and her music. 　☐

a I'd like to learn Portuguese.
b I promise to do it later.
c I hope to win the match.
d I want to get tickets to her concert.
e We're planning to go there on vacation.
f ~~I'm learning to drive.~~
g We need to buy a new one.
h I decided to wear the red one.

3 PRONUNCIATION sentence stress

a <u>Underline</u> the stressed words.

1 **A** Would you like to drive a sports car?
   B Yes, I'd love to.
   A Why?
   B Because I love cars, and I love driving.
2 **A** Would you like to ride a horse?
   B No, I wouldn't.
   A Why not?
   B Because I don't like horses.
3 **A** Do you want to learn to cook?
   B Yes, I need to.
   A Why?
   B Because I want to live on my own.

b **iChecker** Listen and check. Then listen and repeat the dialogues.

4 LISTENING

a 🖉 **iChecker** Listen to a TV host interviewing three people about things they want to do with their lives. What are their ambitions?

1 Dave _____

2 Carolina _____

3 Eddie _____

b 🖉 **iChecker** Listen again and write T (true) or F (false).

1 Dave had a bicycle when he was younger. ___
2 Dave isn't a father. ___
3 Carolina is planning to visit Canada with her sister. ___
4 Carolina enjoys flying. ___
5 Eddie has tickets to see his favorite band in concert. ___
6 Kings of Leon isn't touring this year. ___

USEFUL WORDS AND PHRASES

Learn these words and phrases.

ambitions /æmˈbɪʃnz/
recipes /ˈrɛsəpiz/
preferably /ˈprɛfərəbli/
serious /ˈsɪriəs/
translate /ˈtrænsleɪt/
be yourself /bi yərˈsɛlf/
bite your nails /baɪt yɔr ˈneɪlz/
(see a band) live /laɪv/
stay awake /steɪ əˈweɪk/

---

5 READING

a Read the text. Answer the questions with **J** (Julio), **K** (Kimberley), **Y** (Yusuke), or **G** (Greg).

Things I want to do

Julio, 25, Brazil

I'd love to be in Times Square in New York City at midnight on New Year's Eve! And I'd like it to be snowing, too – that's more romantic. People say that the atmosphere there is amazing. I think it would be a great experience.

Kimberly, 31, Canada

I want to visit the Amazon rainforest. It's such a unique and fascinating place, and I'm really interested in the wildlife that lives there. I'd like to do a trek and go camping there for three weeks or so. I've seen a lot of movies about explorers, and now I'd like to do something really exciting myself.

Yusuke, 26, Japan

What I want to do is go on a road trip across Europe with my two best friends. I've been to the US and Canada, but I've never been to Europe. I want to see all the famous tourist sites like the Eiffel Tower, Big Ben, and the Leaning Tower of Pisa. I read about them in books when I was a child – it would be a dream come true for me to see them in real life.

Greg, 34, the US

It's not very original, but I'd like to drive a really expensive sports car up the coast of California with my wife next to me in the passenger seat. However, right now I own a Toyota Corolla, so I may have to wait a few years before I can achieve my dream!

1 Which person became interested in his or her dream when he or she was very young? ☐
2 Who wants to be part of a traditional celebration? ☐
3 Who needs to buy something before he or she can achieve his or her dream? ☐
4 Which person would like some adventure? ☐

b Guess the meaning of the highlighted words. Check the meaning and pronunciation in your dictionary.

11C Men, women, and the Internet

1 GRAMMAR articles

a Correct the mistake in each answer (**B**).

1 **A** Where are the children? **B** They're at the school.
2 **A** What do you do? **B** I'm engineer.
3 **A** Where's the juice? **B** In a refrigerator.
4 **A** What's that? **B** A ID card.
5 **A** How often do you go? **B** Twice the week.
6 **A** What animals do you like? **B** I like the dogs.
7 **A** How did you travel? **B** By a train.
8 **A** Where did you get that? **B** On Internet.

b Complete the text with *the*, *a / an*, or *–*.

Most people think that ¹ ___the___ Internet is a good thing. At ² _____ work, employees can use it to search for ³ _____ information and to send and receive ⁴ _____ emails. At ⁵ _____ home, ⁶ _____ people can use it for entertainment. You can watch ⁷ _____ music videos, listen to ⁸ _____ music, or, play ⁹ _____ latest computer games online. It is also useful for ¹⁰ _____ shopping, and you don't have to go to ¹¹ _____ bank if you have ¹² _____ online banking service. However, there are some dangers because there is ¹³ _____ problem with security. ¹⁴ _____ computer virus can break your computer and ¹⁵ _____ computer hackers can steal your identity.

2 VOCABULARY The Internet

Unscramble the words to complete the sentences.

1 All our hotel rooms have ___wi-fi___ (IW-IF) access.
2 It's cheaper to _____ (PKSEY) than to make a phone call.
3 Do you ever shop _____ (NONELI)?
4 You only need your username and your password to _____ (GOL NI).
5 Do you want to _____ (DLWODNAO) this file?
6 I sometimes forget to include the _____ (TATHCANEMT) in my emails.
7 I need to _____ (RASHEC ROF) some information before I write my report.
8 You can _____ (OGLEGO) the name of the restaurant to find out the address.
9 They're going to _____ (POLUDA) their vacation pictures tonight.

3 PRONUNCIATION word stress

a Underline the stressed syllable in these words.

1 email   network   website
2 address   online   results
3 document   Internet   username
4 attachment   computer   directions

b **iChecker** Listen and check. Then listen and repeat the words.

4 READING

a Read the article. When did the World Wide Web begin? _____

b Read the article again and number the events in the order they happened.

☐ Tim Berners-Lee developed a new computer language.

☐ Americans opened an agency to develop new technology.

☐ They put the new language on the Internet.

1 The Russians sent a satellite into space.

☐ The World Wide Web made the Internet available to all computer users.

☐ The network changed its name to the Internet.

☐ The agency developed a network to connect computers.

☐ Berners-Lee and a colleague used the new language to write a new program.

5 LISTENING

a iChecker Listen to four speakers talking about how they use the Internet. Match speakers 1–4 to the thing they do most often.

Speaker ☐ uses a social network.

Speaker ☐ plays games.

Speaker ☐ does a job.

Speaker ☐ talks to family and friends.

b iChecker Listen again and match the speakers to the sentences A–D.

Speaker 1 ☐   Speaker 3 ☐

Speaker 2 ☐   Speaker 4 ☐

A This person often puts photos on the Internet.

B This person likes his / her job.

C This person uses the Internet to relax.

D This person saves money because of the Internet.

USEFUL WORDS AND PHRASES

Learn these words and phrases.

advice /əd'vaɪs/

both /bəʊθ/

password /'pæswərd/

username /'yuzərneɪm/

book (tickets / hotels) /bʊk/

lose weight /luz 'weɪt/

make transfers /meɪk 'trænsfərz/

online shopping /ɑnlaɪn 'ʃɑpɪŋ/

pay bills /peɪ 'bɪlz/

The story behind the World Wide Web

To find out when the World Wide Web began, we first need to look at the Internet. The origins of the Internet go back to the space race of the 1950s. After the Russians sent the satellite *Sputnik* into space, Americans wanted to develop their own technology further, so they set up ARPA – the Advanced Research Projects Agency. This agency found a way of connecting computers, which they called ARPANET. In 1974, they changed its name to the internetwork or Internet for short.

In 1980, a scientist at CERN, the European Organization for Nuclear Research, wrote a computer program so that he and his colleagues could share their research. The scientist's name was Tim Berners-Lee, and his software was called ENQUIRE. At first, only scientists at CERN could use the program, which contained a new computer language called hypertext. Then, in 1991, he and a colleague wrote a more advanced version of the program which made hypertext available over the Internet. This was the beginning of the World Wide Web, as we know it. The first website and web server was info.cern.ch. Today, there are more than 227 million websites containing over 65 billion web pages.

Over two billion people now use the Internet, which is nearly a third of the world's population.

Practical English Going home

1 VOCABULARY Public transportation

Complete the paragraphs.

1 You can get a taxi or a [1] c*ab* at a taxi
   [2] s_____. People usually give
   the driver a [3] t_____.

2 Before you get a plane, you have to
   [4] ch_____ in online or at the airport.
   Then you go through security to the
   [5] d_____ area. Finally, you
   go to your [6] g_____.

3 You get a subway at a subway [7] st_____.
   First, you get a [8] t_____, and then
   you find the right [9] pl_____.

4 You get a [10] b_____ at a station
   or a stop. You can buy a ticket in advance
   or sometimes you can pay
   the [11] dr_____.

2 GETTING TO THE AIRPORT

Complete the conversations with a sentence in the box.

Can I pay by credit card?
Could you call me a taxi, please?
Could I have a ticket to O'Hare Airport, please?
How much is it?   And could I have a receipt?
Now, please.   One-way, please.
Coach, please.   To Union Station.
---

1 A [1] *Could you call me a taxi, please?*
   B Yes, of course. Where to?
   A [2] _____
   B And when would you like it for?
   A [3] _____

2 A [4] _____
   C That's $18.50, please.
   A Make it $20. [5] _____
   C Yes, of course. Thank you very much, sir.

3 A [6] _____
   D One-way or round-trip?
   A [7] _____
   D Coach or first class?
   A [8] _____
   D That's $18.50.
   A [9] _____
   D Yes, of course.

3 SOCIAL ENGLISH

Match the words to make phrases.

1 I can't | e | a to accept.
2 Thank you | ☐ | b good trip.
3 I'd love | ☐ | c in Rio de Janeiro.
4 I'm so | ☐ | d so much.
5 Have a | ☐ | e believe it!
6 See you | ☐ | f happy.

4 READING

a Read the text about O'Hare International Airport.

O'Hare International Airport

O'Hare International Airport is the second-busiest international airport in the US, and more than 32 million passengers pass through it every year. Below you can find different ways of getting to the airport.

BY CAR
If you're planning to drive to O'Hare Airport, you need to take Interstate I-190 and turn off on Bessie Coleman Drive. The airport is 19 miles from downtown Chicago and takes about 35 minutes during quiet times.

BY BIKE
Ride your bike to O'Hare Airport's Parking Lot E. You can leave your bike in a special bike parking area in this parking lot. Then take the Airport Transit System (ATS) to the terminal buildings.

BY TRAIN
Chicago Transit Authority's Blue Line runs every ten minutes. It takes about an hour to go from Forest Park to O'Hare Airport. A one-way ticket costs $2.25. Students and senior citizens can ride for a reduced price.

BY BUS
Several different bus companies around Chicago operate services to O'Hare Airport. These buses run 24 hours a day and drop you off in front of the terminal buildings. The price for a one-way ticket can be as low as just a few dollars.

BY TAXI
There are more than 15 different taxi companies to call for a ride to O'Hare Airport. The cost of a taxi from downtown Chicago to the airport is about $45, and the trip takes about 30 to 45 minutes depending on traffic.

b How did the following people get to O'Hare Airport?

1 Diego made a phone call.   By __*taxi*__.
2 Vanessa paid $2.25.   By _____.
3 Samantha went from Forest Park.   By _____.
4 Pete went on the Interstate. By _____.
5 Yoshi exercised.   By _____.

c Underline five words or phrases you don't know. Use your dictionary to look up their meaning and pronunciation.

Films should have a beginning, a middle, and an end
– but not necessarily in that order.

Jean-Luc Godard, French movie director

12A Books and movies

1 GRAMMAR present perfect

a Write the sentences with contractions.

1 I have not read *The Pillars of the Earth*.
   I haven't read The Pillars of the Earth.

2 James has not seen this movie before.
   _____

3 They have gone to the movie theater tonight.
   _____

4 She has cried at a lot of movies.
   _____

5 I have bought all the Harry Potter movies.
   _____

6 They have not taken any photos.
   _____

7 He has interviewed a famous actor.
   _____

8 We have not appeared in a movie.
   _____

b Write sentences with the present perfect.

1 she / read / *The Help*
   She's read The Help _____ .

2 we / not see / this show
   We haven't seen this show _____ .

3 my parents / fall asleep
   _____ .

4 Adam / appear / in a movie
   _____ .

5 I / not speak to an actor
   _____ .

6 you / break / the camera
   _____ .

7 Dawn / not cry / at a movie
   _____ .

8 we / not forget / the tickets
   _____ .

c Complete the dialogue.

A ¹ *Have you heard* (you / hear) of John le Carré?

B Yes, I ² _____ (read) some of his books.

A Really? Which books ³ _____ (you / read)

B I ⁴ _____ (read) *The Constant Gardener* recently. It was great!

A ⁵ _____ (you / see) the movie?

B No, but my brother ⁶ _____ (see) it. He loves John le Carré.

A ⁷ _____ (he / read) *Tinker, Tailor, Soldier, Spy*?

B Yes, and he ⁸ _____ (see) the movie.

2 VOCABULARY irregular past participles

a Write the simple past forms and past participles of these irregular verbs in the chart.

Infinitive	Simple past	Past participle
1 be	*was / were*	*been*
2 break		
3 do		
4 eat		
5 fall		
6 forget		
7 go		
8 leave		
9 sing		
10 speak		
11 take		
12 wear		

b Use past participles from the chart in **a** to complete the sentences.

1 Have you ever ___sung___ karaoke?

2 We've never _____ the movie theater before the end of a movie.

3 My sister has never _____ octopus before.

4 Has your brother ever _____ your birthday?

5 Have you ever _____ glasses?

6 I've never _____ my leg.

7 My friend hasn't _____ the homework.

3 PRONUNCIATION sentence stress

a **iChecker** Listen and <u>underline</u> the stressed words.

> **A** Have you read *The Millennium Trilogy*?
> **B** No, I haven't.
> **A** Have you seen the movies?
> **B** Yes, I have. I've seen all of them.

b **iChecker** Listen again and repeat the sentences. Copy the <u>rhy</u>thm.

4 READING

a Read the article about a movie adaptation of a book. Did fans prefer the ending in the book or the movie?

My Sister's Keeper

Fans of American author Jodi Picoult who have read her novel *My Sister's Keeper* get a big surprise when they see the movie. This is because the movie has a completely different ending from the book.

The novel tells the story of 13-year-old Anna Fitzgerald who was born to save the life of her older sister, Kate, who is very sick. Kate has cancer and Anna goes to hospital many times to give her sister blood and other things to keep Kate alive. However, when Anna is 13, she finds out that Kate needs one of her kidneys, and she decides that she doesn't want to give it to her. Anna goes to find a lawyer to help her fight her case in court.

At the end of the book, Anna wins her case so that in the future she can make her own decisions about her body. Unfortunately, the same day as she wins the case, she is in her lawyer's car when they have a serious accident. Anna is brain-dead after the crash, and the lawyer gives the doctors permission to use Anna's kidney. So in the end, Anna dies and Kate lives.

At the end of the movie, before they know the result of the court case, Kate and Anna's brother, Jesse, tells the family that Kate doesn't want to have any more operations. Kate dies and then Anna's lawyer visits the house to tell Anna she has won the case. So, in the movie Kate dies and Anna lives.

A website asked the people who have read the book and seen the movie to vote on the two different endings. 77% said that they hated the new ending while 13% said they preferred it to the ending in the book. Ten percent said that they enjoyed both the book and the movie and that the ending made no difference to them.

b Read the article again and choose a, b, or c.

1 Jodi Picoult is…
   a a lawyer.
   b a writer.
   c a doctor.
2 Anna's parents had Anna because…
   a they wanted another child.
   b they wanted to save their daughter.
   c they wanted another girl.
3 …dies at the end of the book.
   a The healthy sister
   b The sister who was sick
   c The brother
4 … dies at the end of the movie.
   a The healthy sister
   b The sister who was sick
   c The brother
5 … of the people who voted didn't think the ending was important.
   a 77%
   b 13%
   c 10%

5 LISTENING

a **iChecker** Listen to a radio program. Who wrote the two books? _____

b **iChecker** Listen again. Write T (true) or F (false).

1 *Great Expectations* was made in 1956.   *F*
2 The movie critic is going to talk about two movies. __
3 *Great Expectations* is a black and white movie.   __
4 The main character in *Great Expectations* is a girl. __
5 The movie is more frightening than the book.   __
6 The host has read the book *The English Patient*.   __
7 The author of *The English Patient* isn't American. __
8 The main character in *The English Patient* had a car crash. __
9 The critic says that the best thing about the movie is the love story. __
10 Both the book and the movie have won important prizes. __

USEFUL WORDS AND PHRASES

Learn these words and phrases.

blood /blʌd/
appear /əˈpɪr/
at least /ət ˈlist/
fall asleep /fɔl əˈslip/
How about…? /ˈhaʊ əbaʊt/
order pizza /ˈɔrdər ˈpitsə/

I want to go somewhere I have never been, and I'd like to go there with you.

From The Hitchhiker's Guide to the Galaxy *by Douglas Adams, British writer*

12B I've never been there!

1 GRAMMAR present perfect or simple past?

a Complete the dialogues with the correct form of the verbs in parentheses.

1 **A** _Have you been_ (you / be) on vacation recently?
  B Yes, we have. We _____ (go) to the beach in July.

2 **A** When _____ (your brother / buy) his motorcyle?
  B Last week. My parents _____ (pay) for it.

3 **A** _____ (you / meet) your sister's new roommate?
  B Yes, I _____ (meet) her at a party last month.

4 **A** _____ (you / be) to New York?
  B Yes, I _____ (go) there last year.

5 **A** _____ (your parents / ever / give) you an expensive present?
  B Yes, I _____ (get) a car for my last birthday.

6 **A** Why _____ (he / send) his wife some flowers yesterday?
  B Because he _____ (forget) their anniversary.

b Complete the sentences with *gone* or *been*.

1 Has Clare __*gone*__ home? She isn't at her desk.
2 Have you ever _____ to Disneyland?
3 My sister isn't here because she's _____ for a walk.
4 My neighbors are away because they've _____ on vacation.
5 You look tan. Have you_____ to the beach?
6 It's late so the children have _____ to bed.
7 The refrigerator is full because we've _____ shopping.
8 Have you ever _____ to an Indian restaurant?
9 My best friend has never _____ abroad.
10 Jane's parents are out. They've _____ to the supermarket.

2 PRONUNCIATION irregular past participles

a Circle the word with a different vowel sound.

1 fish	2 saw	3 egg	4 up	5 train	6 phone
given	walk	left	come	taken	broken
written	call	heard	done	made	known
seen	ball	said	drunk	read	lost
driven	last	sent	got	paid	spoken

b iChecker Listen and check. Then listen and repeat the words.

3 VOCABULARY more irregular past participles

a Write the simple past forms and past participles of these irregular verbs in the chart.

	Infinitive	Simple past	Past participle
1	buy	*bought*	*bought*
2	drink		
3	find		
4	give		
5	have		
6	hear		
7	know		
8	lose		
9	make		
10	meet		
11	pay		
12	send		
13	spend		
14	think		
15	win		

b Complete the sentences with past participles from the chart in **a**.

1 I'm going to be late. I've __*lost*__ the car keys.
2 Have you ever _____ long hair?
3 Debbie and Fernando have _____ a new house.
4 Kenji can't go out because he's _____ all his money.
5 My parents have never _____ of Maroon 5.
6 You've _____ a lot of mistakes.
7 She's _____ some money in the street.
8 He's _____ a lot of water today because it's so hot.

4 READING

a Read the email. Check (√) the places Jessica has been to.

_____ Arizona
_____ California
_____ Colorado
_____ New Mexico
_____ Oklahoma
_____ Texas

From: Jessica
To: Brianna
Subject: Hi from the US Southwest!

Dear Brianna,

Thanks for your email telling me all the news from home. I'm glad everyone is well and that you're not missing me too much!

We're more than half way through our trip around the US Southwest, and we're having a great time. We've stayed in four states so far, and now we're in Colorado. We spent three days in San Diego, California where we walked on the 3-mile long Mission Beach Boardwalk along the ocean. From San Diego, we drove to Las Vegas, Nevada where we spent two days seeing the sights. We even saw a show by Cirque du Soleil—an amazing live music, dancing, and circus show—in one of Las Vegas's many theaters. Our next stop was Phoenix, Arizona, which we found too hot—it was over 100 degrees Fahrenheit during the day. The best part of our visit was the Musical Instrument Museum, which has musical instruments from all over the world. From Phoenix we drove to Santa Fe, New Mexico, where we decided to relax and enjoy a spa. The weather was hot in Santa Fe, but not as hot as Phoenix! We wanted to stay longer, but it was time for us to drive to Colorado. And now here we are in Denver. Denver is a beautiful place with a lot of tall, modern buidlings. We've been to the Denver Zoo today, but unfortunately, it rained—just our luck.

We have one more day in Denver, and then we're going to drive to Tulsa. We haven't been to Oklahoma or Texas yet, so we're looking forward to the last part of our trip.

I'll write again when we get to Austin. Until then, take care and give my love to Mom and Dad.

Love,

Jessica

b Read the email again. Where did Jessica…?

1 see dancers _____
2 visit a museum _____
3 have a relaxing time _____
4 take a long walk _____
5 see animals _____

5 LISTENING

a **iChecker** Listen to four speakers talking about different places they have been to. Where did they go? When?

	Where?	**When?**
Speaker 1	_____	_____
Speaker 2	_____	_____
Speaker 3	_____	_____
Speaker 4	_____	_____

b **iChecker** Listen again. Who…?

1 did an extreme sport   Speaker ☐
2 was in a dangerous situation   Speaker ☐
3 took part in a local celebration Speaker ☐
4 wasn't on vacation   Speaker ☐

USEFUL WORDS AND PHRASES

Learn these words and phrases.

recently /ˈrɪsntli/
romantic /roʊˈmæntɪk/
Let's forget it. /lɛts fərˈgɛt ɪt/
TV series /ti ˈvi sɪriz/
win (a cup or medal) /wɪn/

One Ring to rule them all, One Ring to find them,
One Ring to bring them all and in the darkness bind them.
From The Fellowship of the Ring *by J. R. R. Tolkien, British author*

12C The *American English File* questionnaire

1 GRAMMAR review

a Correct the mistakes in the second sentence.

1 Those are her children. They is very young.
   They are very young.

2 Jim lives in the city center. Your apartment is big.
   _____.

3 I went shopping yesterday. I bought a shirt new.
   _____.

4 That's Sophie. She's the sister of Ryan.
   _____.

5 We love the summer. We go on vacation on August.
   _____.

6 Tanya is going to lose her job. She always is late.
   _____.

7 I don't like karaoke. I can't to sing.
   _____.

8 My brother is late. I'm waiting for he.
   _____.

9 We're doing the housework. We don't mind clean.
   _____.

10 Our yard is small. There aren't some plants.
   _____.

11 The hotel was full. There was a lot of guests.
   _____.

12 They're very healthy. They don't eat many sugar.
   _____.

13 I'm 21. I'm more older than you.
   _____.

14 I don't like crocodiles. They're the more dangerous animals.
   _____.

15 Hannah likes languages. She speaks Chinese good.
   _____.

16 My sister has a good job. She's engineer.
   _____.

b Look at the **time expressions** and complete the sentences with the correct form of the verbs. Use the simple present, present continuous, simple past, present perfect, or *be going to*.

1 We **never** _have_ pizza for dinner. (have)
2 Caitlin _____ the dog for a walk **twice a day**. (take)
3 _____ you _____ your friends **last weekend?** (see)
4 They _____ **tomorrow** because Jack is sick. (not come)
5 _____ you **ever** _____ to South America? (be)
6 _____ your son _____ to drive **next year?** (learn)
7 We _____ meat **every day**. (not eat)
8 We _____ a movie **next Saturday**. (see)

9 _____ you **ever** _____ a famous person? (meet)
10 **Last night** my husband _____ dinner. (cook)
11 I think it _____ **tonight**. (rain)
12 What time _____ you **usually** _____ to bed on the weekend? (go)
13 My brother _____ soccer **right now**. (play)
14 We _____ to work **yesterday**. (not walk)
15 What _____ your daughter _____ **today?** (do)
16 I _____ **never** _____ that book, but I'd like to. (read)

2 VOCABULARY review: word groups

a Circle the word that is different.

1 Canada   (Japanese)   Turkey   China
2 Iran   Vietnam   Asia   Mexico
3 tall   expensive   dark   slim
4 lawyer   teacher   shower   waiter
5 aunt   daughter   niece   brother
6 spring   cloudy   snowy   windy
7 fireplace   cupboard   sofa   kitchen
8 mushroom   strawberries   onion   peas
9 pharmacy   department store   bridge   shopping mall

b Continue the series.

1 one, two, three, _four_
2 ten, twenty, _____
3 Monday, Tuesday, _____
4 first, second, _____
5 morning, afternoon, _____
6 once, twice, _____
7 summer, fall, _____
8 June, July, _____
9 second, minute, _____
10 day, week, _____

c Complete the phrases with verbs.

1 _listen_ to music
2 d_____ homework
3 s_____ hello
4 t_____ a shower
5 g_____ shopping
6 t_____ photos
7 h_____ a noise
8 g_____ dressed
9 h_____ two children
10 u_____ a computer

3 PRONUNCIATION review: sounds

a Circle the word with a different sound.

fish	1	rich dirty big
tree	2	bread peas meat
cat	3	safe black fat
car	4	dark day far
clock	5	money model doctor
saw	6	mall more met
bull	7	cook food good
boot	8	who do go
bird	9	tired thirsty nurse
egg	10	eat healthy breakfast
train	11	paid steak said
bike	12	buy nice ring

b iChecker Listen and check.

c Underline the stressed syllable.

1 hos|pi|tal
2 ex|pen|sive
3 ma|ga|zine
4 head|phones
5 ad|mi|ni|stra|tor
6 en|gi|neer
7 I|tal|ian
8 Au|gust
9 di|ffi|cult
10 mu|si|cian
11 ga|rage
12 ba|na|nas

d iChecker Listen and check.

4 READING

Read the article and answer the questions.

THE MOVIES in *The Lord of the Rings* trilogy have had a big impact on New Zealand. The country has become "Middle Earth" to many of the people who have seen the movies. This comes as no surprise to the movie director Peter Jackson, who is in fact a New Zealander. He chose his home country because he knew that the variety of different landscapes made New Zealand the best place to shoot the movies.

Jackson and his team looked over the whole country for the most beautiful and most appropriate areas. The rolling hills of Matamata became Hobbiton, the village where Bilbo Baggins lives, and the volcanic region of Mount Ruapehu transformed into the fiery Mount Doom, where Sauron first made the Ring. In total, the team used 150 different locations all over New Zealand, and they spent 274 days filming.

Thirty of the locations Jackson used are national parks or conservation sites, so he needed to get special permission to film here. In some cases, a special team dug up the protected plants and took them to special nurseries, where they lived until filming finished. Then the team took them back to the park and replanted them again. In Queenstown, Jackson used enormous red rugs to protect the plants in the battle scenes because there were up to 1,100 people on set every day.

The *Lord of the Rings* movies have been so popular that the tourist industry in New Zealand has grown dramatically. Today, tour companies offer a wide range of tours to different locations of the movie, including Hobbiton, Mount Doom, and Edoras.

1 Who directed *The Lord of the Rings* movies?
2 Where is the director from?
3 Why did he choose New Zealand?
4 Which area did they use to create Mount Doom?
5 How many different locations did they use in total?
6 What was the problem with some of the locations?
7 How did they solve the problem?
8 Which locations from the movies can tourists visit today?

5 LISTENING

iChecker Listen to an advertisement for a day trip and complete the notes.

Lord of the Rings Edoras Tour			
Departure time:	Christchurch ¹ 9 a.m.	Lunch:	luxury ⁵_____
Return time:	Christchurch ²_____	Price:	
Transportation:	by ³_____	Adults:	⁶ $_____
Destination:	Mount ⁴_____ (Edoras)	Children:	⁷ $_____

Listening

1 A 🔊

1
Nick Hello.
Sophie Hi, Nick.
Nick Hi, Sophie.
Sophie Nick, what's Sarah's phone number?
Nick Um…it's 917-555-6542.
Sophie Thank you!

2
Receptionist OK…your class on Tuesday is with Paul, and it's in room two. Your class on Thursday is with Kate, and it's in room five.
Student OK, so Thursday is in room three, and Tuesday in room five?
Receptionist No – it's Tuesday in room two, and Thursday in room five.

3
Liz A cheese sandwich and a coffee, please.
Barista That's five dollars and twenty cents, please. Thank you.
Liz Thank you.
Barista Have a nice day!

1 B 🔊

1 **A** Are you Russian?
   B No, I'm Turkish. I'm from Istanbul.
2 **A** Where are you from?
   B We're American. We're from California. We're on vacation in South America.
3 **A** Where's he from? Is he Spanish?
   B No, he isn't. He's from Mexico. He's from Cancún.
4 **A** Mmmm, delicious. Is it French?
   B No, it isn't. It's Italian.

1 C 🔊

R = Receptionist, **E** = Erik
R Good morning. Can I help you?
E Oh, yes. Hello. I have a reservation.
R OK. What's your name?
E Erik.
R Is that Eric with a C?
E No, it's with a K. E-R-I-K.
R OK. And how do you spell your last name?
E T-A-Y-L-O-R
R Can you repeat that please?
E Yes, of course. Sorry. T-A-Y-L-O-R.
R Thanks. Now just a few questions, Mr. Taylor. Where are you from?
E I'm from Florida in the United States.
R Where in Florida?
E Miami.
R Miami. OK. And what's your address?
E It's 15 Atkinson Road.
R What's your zip code?
E Sorry?
R The zip code. You know, a number?
E Ah, yes. It's 33156.
R 33156. Great. What's your email address?
E It's eriktaylor@mail.com.
R And what's your phone number?
E My phone number in Miami is 305 – that's the code for Florida – 555-5692.
R 305-555-5692.

E Yes, that's right. And my cell phone number is 305-555-5701.
R 305-555-5701. OK, thanks Mr. Taylor. Here's your keycard. You're in room 503 on the third floor. Enjoy your stay.
E Thank you very much.

2 A 🔊

Speaker 1 My bag is very important to me because I have my laptop in it! I also have some files and a pen. Um, I have my cell phone, my wallet, and my keys in my pocket, and I sometimes have a newspaper in my bag.
Speaker 2 Well, in my bag I have, uh, my books for the day, um, some pens and pencils to write with, and a file with lots of paper. Oh, and I have my iPod and my headphones too, so I can listen to music.
Speaker 3 What's in my bag? Well, yeah, I have my sunglasses and my camera. And I have a guidebook with a map. Oh, and I have a Spanish-English dictionary, too, to help me understand the people.
Speaker 4 I have a different bag every day, sometimes it's red, sometimes it's white, it depends. But I always have the same things: some tissues, um, the keys to my desk, uh, my wallet of course, and, uh, sometimes a magazine to read.

2 B 🔊

1 He's a Hollywood star, but he isn't American. He's very tall and slim. He's about 54 or 55, I think, but he's still very attractive. He has short brown hair and brown eyes. He's an actor.
2 She's young and she isn't very tall. She's usually slim, but it depends. Her hair is really brown, but it's blond in her music videos. She's American and she's a singer.
3 This actor isn't very tall, but he's very strong. He has short dark hair and dark eyes. He's American and I think he's 70 years old.
4 She's about 54 or 55 now and she's very tall and slim. She has blond hair, sometimes long and sometimes short, and green eyes. She's a British actress and she's in some of the Harry Potter movies.
5 He's a British singer and musician. He's about 62 or 63 now, I think. He's really slim. He has short blond hair, and blue eyes. He is also an actor.

2 C 🔊

1 **A** I'm bored.
   B Me, too.
   A I know! Let's watch a DVD.
   B Good idea.
   A We can watch the new Batman movie.
   B OK.
   A Turn on the TV. OK, now…where's the movie?
2 **A** I'm hungry.
   B Are you?
   A Yes, I am. Is the restaurant open?
   B No, it isn't. It's only five o'clock.
   A Oh.
   B Let's call reception. We can ask for some sandwiches.
   A Great idea! Give me the phone.

3 **A** I'm hot.
   B Turn on the air conditioning, then.
   A It's already on.
   B Is it? OK, then let's open the windows.
   A Are we there yet?
   B Yes, we are. Don't worry. It's only another 4 miles.
4 **B** I'm not hungry.
   A Why not?
   B I'm stressed. I have a lot of problems at work.
   A Relax! It's the weekend. Let's go for a long walk and you can tell me all about it.
   B Great.
   A Finish your salad and we can go.
   B OK. Let's pay the bill.
5 **A** I'm tired.
   B I know. It's very late.
   A What time is our plane?
   B At 11:15 p.m. That's another hour to wait.
   A An hour!
   B Yes. Come on. Let's have a coffee. It might wake us up.

3 A 🔊

Hannah I like the parks in Britain, especially Hyde Park in London. The parks are clean and some are really big, and it's great to go for a walk and see so many trees and plants in the middle of a city. There is always something interesting to see or do, too. Sometimes there are festivals where you can hear music or watch a movie. But I can also relax, and read a newspaper on a Sunday morning.
   But, I don't like the food here – it's very expensive, and I can't find good Korean food!
Lina In Britain, I think that people are very friendly and polite. At work, it's relaxed, and my colleagues always help me when I have a question or a problem. I also really like the buildings in Britain; the old buildings are very beautiful.
   What don't I like about Britain? There are a lot of people and there's a lot of traffic, especially in London. It's difficult to relax.
Julianna What I really like about Britain is that it's really easy to meet people from all over the world. It's very international, and I think that most people are friendly to people from other countries. I also really like eating food from different parts of the world – in Britain you can try food from every country!
   I think it's difficult to make friends in Britain. People like to help and are very polite, but it can take a long time to become friends with British people.

3 B 🔊

H = Host, **J** = James, **M** = Maria, **F** = Frank
H Good evening and welcome to *What's Your Job?* And our team tonight is Maria, who's a lawyer…
M Good evening.
H …and Frank, who's an actor.
F Good evening.
H And our first guest tonight is…
J James.

H Hello, James. OK team, you have one minute to ask James questions about his job, starting now. Let's have your first question.

M James, do you make things?

J No. No, I don't.

F James, do you have a college degree?

J Yes, I do.

M Do you speak any foreign languages?

J No, I don't need any foreign languages.

F Do you wear a uniform?

J Well, it's not really a uniform, but I wear a white coat, yes.

M Do you travel?

J Uh, I don't go to different countries, but I drive to people's houses sometimes.

F Do you earn a lot of money?

J Do I earn a lot of money? Well, I think the money is very good, yes.

H You only have time for one more question, team.

M Do you work with other people?

J Well, I work with one other person, but my job isn't really about people…

H Time is up. OK, team. So, what's James's job?

3 C))

J = Jessica, **M** = Max

J Hi. Are you Max?

M Yes. Are you Jessica?

J Yes, I am.

M Nice to meet you. Well, let's go in and sit down. Do you like sushi?

J Yes. I love Japanese food. It's my favorite.

M Good. So, Jessica, what do you do?

J I'm a flight attendant.

M Really? That's incredible?

J Why?

M Because I'm a pilot!

J Oh! You're right. That is incredible! Which airline do you work for?

M United. And you?

J Jet Blue. I love my job.

M Me too. What do you do on the weekends, Jessica?

J I meet my friends. We go to the movies or to a restaurant. How about you?

M I like the movies, too. What kind of movies do you like?

J I like comedies more than anything.

M Me too. Who's your favorite actor?

J Johnny Depp. I love him!

M Yes, he's good, isn't he? Do you live near the movie theater?

J Yes, there's a movie theater near my house.

M When do you go there?

J I go on Saturday evenings.

M Let's go together next Saturday.

J OK. What do you want to see?

4 A))

A = Angie, **J** = Jessie

A Who's that?

J That's my nephew.

A Is that your sister's son or your brother's son?

J My brother's.

A How old is your nephew? He looks young.

J He's 13. The photo is from his birthday last week.

A Let's see the next one. Is that your family, too?

J Yes, it is. That's my sister.

A Wow! She's really tall.

J Yes, she plays basketball. She's very good.

A That's a beautiful beach. Where is it?

J It's a beach in California – I can't remember the name. I love it there!

A Is this California, too?

J No, it isn't. It's a music festival in Canada.

A Are those girls in your family?

J No, they aren't. They're friends from college.

A Who's the blond one?

J That's Rosie. We live in the same apartment.

A Who's the boy?

J He's Rosie's boyfriend. I don't like him very much, but she doesn't see him often.

A Are there any more?

J Yes. Look at this one.

A You look great! And who's that sitting next to you?

J He's my boyfriend, Pete. It's the office party from last year.

A He's good-looking. Does he work with you?

J Well, sort of…He's the manager!

4 B))

I = Interviewer, **M** = Mark

I What do you do, Mark?

M I'm a taxi driver.

I Do you work at night or during the day?

M I work at night.

I What time do you start work?

M At about seven o'clock in the evening. I stop for a break at about two o'clock and I have something to eat.

I What do you have?

M A hamburger or a pizza and a soda. I'm really hungry at that time.

I What time do you finish work, Mark?

M I go home at about six o'clock in the morning and I go to bed immediately. I sleep for about eight hours and then I get up and have breakfast.

I What do you do in the afternoon?

M I go to the gym for an hour or so, and then I take a shower. After that, I watch TV or check my emails until I have dinner.

I What time is that?

M At six o'clock. Then I get into my car and start work again.

I Do you like your job?

M Yes, I love it.

I Thank you for your time, Mark.

M You're welcome.

4 C))

H = Host, **M** = Marge,

R = Robbie, **D** = Dr. Atkins

H Hello, and welcome to *Who's Healthy?* Today we have Marge Wilson and her son, Robbie, with us. Marge, do you think you're healthy?

M Um, yes. I think so.

H And what about you, Robbie? Are you healthy?

R Of course!

H Well, I'm going to ask you some questions and we're going to find out *Who's healthy?* First of all, Marge. How old are you, Marge?

M I'm 48.

H OK. So, how often do you eat fast food, Marge?

M Never. I don't like it.

H OK. And how often do you have breakfast?

M I always have breakfast. I have a cup of tea and some cereal.

H Good. And how often do you do exercise?

M I go to the gym three times a week.

H OK, and how many hours do you usually sleep?

M Well, I get up early, and I always go to bed early, too. I usually sleep for about eight hours.

H That's great, Marge. And now it's Robbie's turn. Robbie, how old are you?

R Twenty.

H And how often do you eat fast food?

R Well, I love pizza and hamburgers, and I sometimes have French fries, so yeah, I eat fast food about five times a week.

H What about breakfast? How often do you have breakfast?

R I don't have time because I always get up late, so…I hardly ever have breakfast.

H OK, and how often do you exercise?

R Oh, I do a lot of exercise. I play soccer four times a week.

H Good. That's better. And how many hours do you usually sleep?

R I'm not sure. I go to bed late because I'm on my computer, so I guess I sleep for about six hours.

H OK. Thank you, Robbie. And now it's time to see what the doctor thinks. Dr. Atkins, Who's healthy? Marge? Robbie? Or both of them?

D Well, Marge always has breakfast and she never eats fast food. She often exercises and she gets a lot of sleep. So, Marge, you're right. You're very healthy!

H And what about Robbie?

D Well, Robbie exercises four times a week, but he often eats fast food and he never has breakfast. He doesn't sleep enough either. So Robbie, you're wrong. You aren't very healthy.

H So, there you have it everyone. A healthy mom and an unhealthy son! And that's all we have time for today. Join us again tomorrow at the same time for *Who's healthy?*

5 A))

1 **A** Let's go to the swimming pool on the weekend.

   B OK. Can we go on Saturday? I'm busy on Sunday.

   A Yes, but I always play tennis in the morning. Let's go in the afternoon.

   B OK. See you there.

2 **A** I want to have lunch in this restaurant. Can I park here?

   B No, sir, you can't.

   A What about outside the movie theater?

   B No parking spaces there. A lot of people leave their cars outside the hospital. You can park there.

   A Thanks.

3 **A** Can you help me with my homework?

   B Not now, sorry.

   A Can you help me after lunch?

   B No. I'm busy.

   A When can you help me?

   B After dinner. I don't have any plans tonight.

4 **A** Let's write a postcard to Chris. Do you have a pen?

   B Yes. Here you are.

   A What about a stamp?

   B We can buy a stamp in the store.

   A OK. Do you know her address?

   B No. Do you?

   A No, I don't!

5 **A** OK. Let's go in.

   B Sorry. We can't.

   A Why not? Is your boss here?

   B No, I can't hear him. But it isn't that. It's the door!

   A Oh, now I understand. You can't open it.

   B No! I don't know where my keys are!

5 B))

Speaker 1 They both work, so it starts when they leave home in the morning. I don't know how many they have – three, four, five – but they make a terrible noise. They take them out for a walk in the evening, so it's nice and quiet then, but they sometimes go out at night and the noise starts again. I don't know why people have animals when they're never at home.

Speaker 2 It's really bad. They do it every Friday and Saturday night. The music starts at about eight o'clock and then we hear the cars. They park outside my house and soon the street is full of cars. The problem is that they don't stay in the house – they go out in the yard to dance, too. They don't leave until about six in the morning, so we don't sleep all night.

Speaker 3 They're really nice people, actually. He's a lawyer and she's a doctor. The problem is what they do in their free time. They both finish work early, so they're home by five o'clock. We can't watch TV or listen to our own music because we can't hear it. They play the piano and violin all evening. It's so noisy!

Speaker 4 I'm so tired right now. Every time I go to sleep, he starts… I know my neighbors love their son, and he's only three months old, but I wish he wouldn't wake up all the time. I thought babies sleep and eat all the time. He's changed my neighbors' lives, and he's changed mine, too!

 5 C

Tour 1: Butchart Gardens
These gardens were planted in 1904 by Jennie Butchart. Walk around the gardens or take a boat ride to see the beautiful flowers. You can also listen to bands play many different types of music.

Tour 2: Emily Carr House
This is the home of famous Canadian writer and artist, Emily Carr. Take a tour of the house and see Emily's paintings and other beautiful works of art. Listen to stories about the artist's life in the late 1800's.

Tour 3: Beacon Hill Park
The park is the biggest in Victoria. It's a very nice place to visit with your family. It has a zoo where children can touch animals and a lot of places to play sports like tennis and soccer.

Tour 4: The Victoria Bug Zoo
This zoo only has two rooms. It's small because it only has insects! Walk around with a tour guide and see how very small insects like ants live!

Tour 5: The University of Victoria
The university was built in 1902. Famous students include artists and politicians. The library has over 2 million books.

Tour 6: Hatley Castle
This castle is a beautiful old building with an interesting history. The castle is now part of a college. It's also famous because it's Professor Xavier's school in the *X-Men* movies.

Tour 7: The Empress Hotel
This hotel is near the water and has 477 rooms, 4 restaurants, and an indoor swimming pool. It is famous for its afternoon tea service.

Tour 8: Art Gallery of Greater Victoria
This gallery has many paintings and drawings by Canadian artists. It also has a lot of important art like a Chinese bell from 1641.

6 A

H = Holly, **B** = Beth, **E** = Emily
H Hello, Emily. It's Holly.
B It isn't Emily. It's Beth. I'm Emily's sister.
H Oh. Hello. Um, is Emily there?
B No, I'm sorry. She's taking the dog for a walk.
H Oh. Well. Can you give her a message?
B Yes, of course.
H Can you tell her my bag is in her car and I need it?
B Oh. Your bag. OK. Does she have your number?
H I don't know.

B OK. Wait a minute. I need a pen. OK. What's your number?
H It's 606-555-4923.
B That's 606-555-4923.
H Yes, that's right.
B Wait a minute, Holly. Don't go, I think Emily is opening the door. Emily? It's for you.
E What? Oh, the phone. Hello?
H Hi, Emily. It's Holly.
E Oh, hi, Holly. How are you?
H I'm fine. Listen. My bag's in your car.
E Is it?
H Yes. And my keys are in the bag, and I can't open the door of my apartment. My cell phone's in my bag too, so I'm calling from the apartment next door. Can you give me my bag?
E Oh, right. Yes. Yes, of course.
H Let's meet in the cafe near my house.
E OK.
H Thanks, Emily.
E No problem. See you in a minute.
H Bye.

6 B

Speaker 1 My favorite day of the year is New Year's Day. I always feel positive when I wake up, and I love staying in bed for an hour or so, thinking about my plans for the next year. I like knowing that I can forget the disasters of the year before and just start again.

Speaker 2 I love waking up on the first day of my summer vacation. It's wonderful going somewhere new and you don't know anything about it. I don't like packing, though, so I always get my bags ready the night before. Then I can enjoy every second of my trip.

Speaker 3 My birthday is in the fall, which is probably why I love this season. I try to go to a park or the countryside at least once a week in the fall to see the beautiful colors of the trees. But I hate it when it rains and the leaves get wet and slippery!

Speaker 4 I hate being inside in the winter, especially when it gets dark at four o'clock, so I'm always waiting for spring to come. I love seeing the new spring flowers on one of those typical spring days, when it's cold but sunny. I love photography, and I often go out and take pictures of trees and flowers.

6 C

1 A What kind of music do you like, Raul?
B I don't know. I like all kinds, really.
A Well, do you like heavy metal?
B Oh, no! That's too loud for me.
A What about reggae?
B No. Reggae's too slow.
A Well, what <u>do</u> you like?
B I usually listen to rock, so that's probably my favorite.

2 A Do you have a favorite CD?
B Yes. Yes, I do. I always listen to it in the car.
A Which group is it by?
B Well, it's not really by a group. It's sung by actors.
A Oh. Is it from a movie?
B Yes. It's the soundtrack from *Mamma Mia!* I love it!
A Isn't that about ABBA?
B Yes and no…It's a musical, with the songs by ABBA, but the actors in the movie sing them.
A I see…

3 A How do you usually listen to music, Wendy?
B Well, I don't listen to the radio, that's one thing for sure. I want to hear music, not the voices of the announcers.
A What about CDs?
B Well, I have a lot of those, but they're in a box in the garage somewhere. I usually listen to music on my laptop. I have a good Internet connection at home and at work, and I can listen to what I want.

4 A Do you want to go to a concert with me next month?
B OK. Who's playing? I hope it isn't Justin Bieber. You know I don't like him.
A No, don't worry. This singer is nothing like him. Anyway, it's a woman.
B Rihanna! Great! I'd love to come.
A No, sorry, it isn't Rihanna. It's Beyoncé.
B Oh. Right. Beyoncé. OK. How much are the tickets?

5 A What do you think of this song, John?
B I don't know. It's very different from her other songs.
A I love it! It's really new and original.
B Yes, but it's slow, and it isn't easy to dance to.
A So you don't like it?
B No, it's OK. But I prefer her other songs.

 7 A

H = Host, **T** = Tom
H Hello, and welcome to what is a very special show, because we're going to find out the results of our poll. Tom Brewer from the Discovery Channel is here to tell us who the greatest American of all time is. Hello, Tom.
T Hi, there.
H So, let's look at the Top 5, Tom.
T All right. Well, number 5 on the list is, in fact, Ben Franklin.
H OK. I'm not surprised.
T I'm not either. Did you know that he was the owner of a newspaper, *The Pennsylvania Gazette*, at the age of 22? Or that he was an expert swimmer?
H No, I didn't know that! Very interesting! But who is number 4?
T Well, number 4 is George Washington.
H Ah, yes…George Washington. Tell us something about him.
T Well, he was born in Virginia on February 22, 1732. He was the first president of the US. He died in 1779 at the age of 67.
H OK. Who's next?
T Number 3 on the list is Martin Luther King, Jr.
H Yes, he was an amazing person.
T That's right. So let me tell you about him. He was born on January 15th, 1929 in Atlanta, Georgia. He was famous because he was one of the leaders of the US civil rights movement. He was killed on April 4th, 1968. He was only 39 years old.
H Yes, that was tragic. So, Number 2?
T Number 2 is Abraham Lincoln, the 12th president of the US.
H Really? Tell us about him.
T Well, he was born on February 12th in 1809. He was president during the American Civil War, and he was killed on April 15th, 1865. He wasn't very old when he died, only 56.
H OK…and now for the moment we've been waiting for. Who is the greatest American of all time? Who is at the top of the list?

T Well, I'll give you a clue. It's a man…he was born on February 6th, 1911 and died in 2004, He was an actor and a US president!

H I knew it! It's Ronald Reagan!

T That's right. Ronald Reagan is the greatest American of all time. Americans voted for Reagan because jobs were good and salaries were high when he was president.

H Tom Brewer, thank you so much for joining us.

T My pleasure.

7 B))

Speaker 1 I had a bad trip one vacation when I wanted to visit my family back home in Chicago. About twenty minutes after leaving the airport, there was a problem with our plane. We returned to the airport again and waited five hours for another plane. Finally, I arrived in Chicago eight hours later than I planned.

Speaker 2 We tried to go on vacation to Toronto one year, but it was a disaster. We started our trip late and stopped for lunch in a town on the way. When we were on the road after lunch, our car started making a strange noise and finally, it stopped altogether. The car ended up in a garage, and we called a taxi to take us home again.

Speaker 3 My bad trip happened when I was in college. I wanted to go home for the weekend, so I was on a train. The trip was very long – about seven hours – and I was almost home. We stopped at the last station before mine, but then we didn't start again. The train was broken. In the end, my dad picked me up in his car.

Speaker 4 I had a bad experience with a bus company once. I booked a ticket from the Port Authority Bus Terminal in New York City to Newark Airport, but there were a lot of people at the bus station when I arrived, and it was impossible to get on the bus. In the end, I traveled to the airport with a businessman in a taxi. He didn't ask me for any money, which was nice.

7 C))

I = Interviewer, **M** = Melissa

I Can you tell us about a memorable night, Melissa?

M Well, let me see. There are a lot of them, actually. But yes, there was one particular night this year that was memorable.

I When was it?

M It was February 14th.

I Valentine's Day?

M Yes. That's why I remember the date. It was Valentine's Day, but I didn't have a boyfriend at the time. In fact, I was with two friends.

I Where were you?

M I was in Miami. There was a concert that night by my favorite singer, Drake, so I traveled to Miami to see it.

I When did you arrive in Miami?

M The night before the concert.

I So, what did you do before the concert?

M We had a coffee at an interesting coffee shop near the beach. Then we tried to find the concert. We didn't know exactly where the theater was, so we drove around for a very long time. In the end, we got there five minutes before the concert started.

I Was the concert good?

M Yes, it was fantastic. Drake sang all our favorite songs, and we danced and sang for about two hours.

I Did you go home after the concert?

M No, we didn't go home right away. We didn't have dinner before it started, so we were hungry.

We went to a fast-food restaurant and had a hamburger. It was delicious! After that, we drove home.

I What time did you get home?

M We didn't get home that late. It was two o'clock in the morning, more or less. But we had a great time. That was the important thing.

8 A))

H = Host, **D** = Detective

H Hello and welcome to *What Next?*, the program that looks at today's career opportunities. In the studio with us is Detective Jeremy Downs from the Metropolitan Police. He's here to tell us about his job and how he got it. Hello, Jeremy.

D Good morning, Peter.

H So, tell us, why did you decide to join the police?

D Well, it runs in my family, really. My dad was a detective, and so was his father. I always knew that this was what I wanted to do.

H What did you need to become a detective?

D First, I got a college degree in criminal justice. Then I had to get experience as a regular police officer. So I worked as a police officer for two years. Then I took two tests – one to test my knowledge of the law and one to test my physical fitness for the job.

H Detective, what do you like most about your job?

D Well, you feel great when you solve a mystery and find a murderer. That's the best thing about it. And also, I'm usually outside or talking to people, so I don't spend much time in an office. I'm never bored when I'm working.

H And what don't you like about it?

D It's a very stressful job. I'm usually working on more than one case at a time, and sometimes it's difficult to know what to do first. And going to the scene of a murder can be terrible. But apart from that, I love my job and I recommend it to anyone who likes finding answers and solving problems.

H Detective Downs, thank you for joining us.

8 B))

M = Mrs. Goodings, **J** = Joanna, **B** = Bradley

M Hello. Good morning. I'm Mrs. Goodings.

J Hi. I'm Joanna, and this is Bradley.

B Hi.

M Hello. Please come in. So…let's start, OK? This is the kitchen, as you can see.

B It's very big.

M Yes. There isn't a dining room, so we eat in here.

J Oh look! The walls are big windows! You can see the yard – it's beautiful!

B Can I ask you a question, Mrs. Goodings? Why did we come in the back door?

M We always use the back door. There isn't a rug in the kitchen so there aren't any problems with dirty shoes.

B Oh. Right.

J Where's the washing machine?

M It's in the corner over there.

J Oh, yes. I see it. Why is there a hole in the ceiling?

M Well, upstairs is the bathroom. The hole is for when you take a shower. You take off your clothes and put them down the hole. They land on the floor next to the washing machine.

J Oh. That's interesting!

M Yes…It was my idea…Now…this way please…I want to show you the living room. There. What do you think?

J Oh! There are big windows here, too. I love it!

B Mrs. Goodings, is there a television?

M No, there isn't. My husband and I don't watch TV. We prefer listening to music. Now…let's go upstairs.

J There are four bedrooms upstairs, is that right?

M Yes. Four bedrooms and a bathroom.

B Is this the bathroom?

M Yes, it is. Be careful with the…

B Aargh!!!

J Bradley? Bradley? Where is he?

M Don't worry. He's in the kitchen.

J What?

M Do you remember the hole in the ceiling?

J Oh, no! Bradley? Bradley? Are you all right?

8 C))

Speaker 1 When I was in Costa Rica, I stayed in a bed-and-breakfast hotel with a difference. It was in the middle of the jungle and we could see monkeys and birds from our window. As well as an air-conditioned bedroom, there was a full bathroom with a warm-water shower. We had a small refrigerator and a coffeemaker, too.

Speaker 2 I spent the night in an ice hotel when I was in the north of Sweden. The temperature in the room was 23°F and the only furniture was a bed made of ice and snow. I slept in a special sleeping bag with all my clothes on – I even wore a hat! It wasn't very comfortable, really, because there wasn't even a bathroom!

Speaker 3 I once stayed in a very artsy hotel when I was in Berlin. All of the rooms in the hotel were completely different. In the middle of my room there was a diamond-shaped bed and when I lay down, I could see hundreds of people who looked just like me. There weren't any cupboards, so I put my bags under the bed.

Speaker 4 I went to Fiji with my husband after we got married and we stayed in a really special hotel. A special elevator took us down to our room, which was surrounded by fish and other sea animals. There was a large, comfortable bed in the bedroom and a library and personal office in the living room. We loved it there!

9 A))

Speaker 1 My favorite meal is roast beef. It sounds boring really – just a piece of meat, but you need to cook it for the right amount of time. My mom cooks it perfectly and she always serves it with roasted potatoes and a lot of other vegetables – peas, carrots, broccoli, and beans. Then she pours a sauce called gravy all over it. Delicious!

Speaker 2 Indian food is really popular these days, and I absolutely love it! We're lucky because we have a great Indian restaurant down the street. My favorite dish is chicken tikka masala, which is chicken in a sauce made with tomatoes, cream, and spices. I always order special Indian bread to eat with it.

Speaker 3 You probably think I'm crazy, but one of my favorite meals is a hot dog and French fries. Yes, I know it's not very healthy, but I only have it about twice a month. I always buy it from the same street vendor, and if the weather's nice, I sit outside in the park to eat it. I put a lot of mustard and relish on the hot dog. Yum!!!

Speaker 4 My favorite food is Chinese food, and I always order the same dish – sweet and sour tofu and vegetables. This is pieces of tofu in a sauce made of sugar, tomatoes, white vinegar, and soy sauce. The sauce also has pineapple, green peppers, and onion in it. I always eat it with rice. I have it at the restaurant, and sometimes I get it to go and eat it at home.

9 B)))

H = Host, **M** = Miriam

H Hello and welcome to the program. Our first guest today is nutritionist Miriam Shepherd. She's here to give us some advice about healthy eating. Miriam, what do we need to eat to be healthy?

M Well, basically, we all need a balanced diet.

H And what exactly is a balanced diet?

M It's when you eat the right amount of food from each of the five different food groups.

H Can you tell us more about those groups, Miriam?

M Yes, of course. Let's start with carbohydrates. These are things like bread, pasta, rice, and potatoes. We need to eat a lot of carbohydrates because they give us energy.

H OK. What's next?

M The next group is fruit and vegetables. Things like apples and oranges, and peas and carrots. These contain important vitamins, so you need to eat something from this group at every meal.

H OK. What's the third group?

M The third group is protein, which is in food like meat and eggs. We need it to grow and to repair the body. You need to eat a lot of foods from this group, but not necessarily with every meal.

H Interesting. What's the next group, Miriam?

M Milk and dairy. Dairy foods are things like cheese and yogurt. This group contains calcium, which is important for our bones and teeth. But you have to be a little careful because they sometimes contain a lot of fat. You need to eat something from this group every day, but not necessarily every meal.

H And which is the last group, Miriam?

M The last group is fats and sugars. These are found in snacks, like cake, cookies, candy, and chips. Fats and sugars aren't very good for you, so only eat a little food from this group – maybe once or twice a week.

H Thank you, Miriam. That was very helpful.

M My pleasure.

9 C)))

M = Michael, **R** = Rachel

M Rachel, did you know that there are two cities called Birmingham?

R Really? I know the one in the state of Alabama in the US, but where's the other one?

M It's in the UK.

R OK. Are the cities very small?

M Not really. One big difference is the population. There are only 243,000 people living in Birmingham in the US, whereas there are over a million in Birmingham in the UK.

R So, Birmingham in the UK is bigger then?

M Well, no. The area of Birmingham in the UK is 63 square miles while Birmingham in the US covers 93.8 square miles.

R Oh, that's big.

M Yes, but there aren't as many people. Birmingham in the UK isn't very green.

R And the American Birmingham is really green.

M Yes. And there's also a big difference in age. Birmingham in the UK was already a small village as early as the seventh century while Birmingham in the US didn't exist until 1871.

R OK. What about the weather? It's always raining over here so the weather is probably better in Birmingham in the UK.

M You're right! There are 26 inches of rain in Birmingham in the UK. There is twice as much in Birmingham in the US—53 inches.

R Interesting!

M Yes, but it's colder over there. The average temperature in Birmingham in the US is 73° F whereas in Birmingham in the UK it's 55° F. That's ten degrees colder.

R So, why are you telling me all this anyway?

M I'm reading an article in the newspaper. It's about a mistake that they made in Birmingham. That's Birmingham in the UK, not ours.

R What happened?

M They made an advertisement for Birmingham in the UK, but they used the wrong photo. They put a photo of Birmingham in the US on the advertisement instead of Birmingham in the UK.

R No! How funny!

M Yes, I thought so, too!

10 A)))

H = Host, **M** = Max

H Hello, and welcome to the travel section of the program. Our guest today is travel writer Max Miller, whose book *Superlative Sights* came out yesterday. Max, welcome to the program.

M Thank you, Gloria.

H So what exactly is your book about?

M Well, it's basically about the biggest, the best, and the most beautiful places in the world.

H Can you give us some examples?

M Yes, of course. Let's start with Ayers Rock in Australia. Its other name is Uluru, and it's the world's largest rock. It's almost 12,000 feet long, 7,920 feet wide, and 1,141 feet high – enormous!

H Yes, I see what you mean. What else?

M How about the world's highest waterfall? Angel Falls in Venezuela is 3,212 feet high. A lot of the water evaporates before it hits the ground.

H Wow! Are there only natural places in your book, or do you have any man-made structures?

M Yes, we include man-made structures, too. For example, do you know what the tallest building is right now?

H No…tell us more.

M Well, it's Burj Khalifa in Dubai in the United Arab Emirates. It stands 2,717 feet high.

H Incredible!

M What about the oldest city in the world?

H I'm not sure. Um…somewhere in Egypt?

M Almost, but not quite. It's Aleppo, in Syria. The city dates back to 600 B.C. and it's the oldest continuously inhabited city in the world.

H Really? I didn't know that.

M There are also some interesting facts about transporation. For instance, do you know anything about the longest train trip?

H Well, I suppose it's in Russia.

M That's right. The Trans-Siberian Railway from Moscow to Vladivostok is 5,771 miles long and crosses seven different time zones.

H That's one long train ride!

M That's right. And how about plane trips? What's the shortest runway in the world?

H Runway? You mean where the planes land at the airport?

M That's right.

H I have no idea.

M Well, it's on the beautiful island of Saba in the Caribbean. The runway is only 1,300 feet long and it ends in a 196-foot drop into the ocean.

H This is fascinating stuff, Max. I can't wait to read your book!

10 B)))

Speaker 1 I had my first experience CouchSurfing in China. I wanted to spend a few days in a city called Guilin, so I made contact with a Chinese guy named Leo. Leo was the perfect host: he gave me a bed, he organized a dinner that other CouchSurfers came to, and he showed me around the city. I loved it, and I'd recommend it to anyone!

Speaker 2 My first CouchSurfing experience did not go well. I was in Boston – in the state of Massachusetts in the US, and I found a college student who agreed to host me. First, he was late and then he didn't stop talking about himself all night. In the end, I said I was tired and went to bed. The next morning, I left Boston and took the train to New York City, where my host was an older woman, and I had a much better time.

Speaker 3 I'm Canadian, and my first CouchSurfing experience was in New Orleans in the state of Louisiana in the US. I wanted to do some research for a novel I'm writing, so I needed to meet as many people as possible. My sister told me about the website, so I decided to try it out. In the end, I stayed with someone different every night, and I got a lot of ideas for my book!

Speaker 4 I was in Australia working when I found out about the CouchSurfing website. I wanted to travel around the country on weekends, but I didn't know anyone. A friend suggested looking at the CouchSurfing website, and I'm very happy that I did. I now have friends all over Australia, and some of them are going to visit me in the US when I go back next month.

10 C)))

P = Pete, **A** = Amy

P Amy, do you remember Uri Geller?

A No, I don't. Who is he?

P He is a kind of psychic. He was on TV a lot in the past and he became famous.

A What kind of tricks did he do?

P Well, his most famous trick was bending spoons. There's a photo here – come and take a look.

A Oh, there's a video here, too, on YouTube. Let's watch it.

P You see? At first, the spoon looks normal. Here, he's touching it with his finger…and now, it's bent.

A That's amazing!

P Actually…it isn't.

A What?

P It's a trick.

A So how does he do it?

P The spoon is bent before he shows it to us. He's hiding the bent part in his hand, so that you think it's a normal spoon. You don't have much time to look at the spoon at all because he's talking so much. What he's doing is distracting you while he's pulling the bent spoon slowly out of his hand. You think he's bending it but, in fact, he isn't.

A So, the guy is a cheater.

P Yes, but he's a very famous cheater.

A Does he still do his trick in public?

P Yes, he does. And the most incredible thing is that people still believe it.

11 A)))

Speaker 1: Toronto, Canada

On the weekend, the city is pretty busy. It's very similar to New York City or Washington, D.C. The streets are crowded with cars and people. There are interesting neighborhoods to visit, great restaurants to eat at, and a lot of places to hear music. I think most people stay in the city because there isn't much to do outside of the city.

People dress nicely here, especially at work. In big companies, it's normal for men to wear suits and women to wear business clothes. On the weekend, people dress more casually. They wear jeans or shorts and T-shirts, depending on the weather.

An interesting thing is that Toronto's nickname is "Hollywood North." A lot of TV and movie companies film their shows in Toronto. The city is also home to the Toronto International Film Festival. Only the Cannes Film Festival in France is bigger!

Speaker 2: Reykjavik, Iceland
In Iceland, a very important part of life is swimming and going to a hot tub, which is like a small swimming pool with hot water. People go before work or on the weekend to meet with their friends, or sometimes even to have business meetings!

The countryside in Iceland is incredible. There are almost no trees, and there are volcanoes and fields of lava, which are the incredibly hot stones that come out of the volcanoes. You can walk for days and not see another person, because there aren't many people in Iceland. In Reykjavik, there are less than 250,000 people, and the second-biggest city has only 15,000.

Icelandic people are very creative. It's normal for many people to make music, paint or draw, and even write books. Also, many people make their own clothes, and they look really fashionable!

11 B))

H = Host, **D** = Dave, **C** = Carolina, **E** = Eddie
H Hello. I'm Jenny Richards, and I'm on the streets of New York City asking people what they want to do with their lives. Let's start with this man over here. Hello.
D Hi.
H I'm Jenny Richards from TV NYC. What's your name?
D I'm Dave.
H OK, Dave, we'd like to ask you about your ambitions for the future. What do you want to do with your life?
D Well, uh, what I'd really like, um, is…
H Yes?
D I'd really like to buy a motorcycle. I had a little dirt bike when I was younger, but I stopped riding it when I got married and had kids. Now, I'd like to start again.
H Well, good luck with your ambition, Dave. Let's talk to someone else now. Hello. What's your name?
C Carolina.
H So, what do you want to do with your life, Carolina?
C Well, I'd love to go traveling to different places.
H Oh really? Any particular place?
C Yes. I'd really like to go to Australia with my sister. I have friends there, and it's a very exciting country.
H Why don't you, then?
C I can't.
H Why not?
C My sister hates flying, and it's a 22-hour flight.
H Well, maybe one day you can go there on your own. Good luck with your ambition, Carolina. Now, what about you? What's your name?
E I'm Eddie.
H Do you have any ambitions, Eddie?
E I'd like to see Kings of Leon live.
H Why Kings of Leon?
E They're my favorite band.
H Why don't you get a ticket for their next concert?
E Yeah, I want to, but they aren't touring this year. They're making a new album.

H Well, maybe next year. Now, let's talk to this woman over here…

11 C))

Speaker 1 I really couldn't live without the Internet. Every evening after dinner, I spend a few hours on my laptop playing games online. My job is very stressful, so it helps me relax. I forget about my problems and focus on something different. I think it's really good for me.

Speaker 2 The Internet is really important for me because I live abroad. All of my family and friends live in the US, and I'm living in the UK. Phone calls are really expensive, but with the Internet I can Skype them whenever I want to. With Skype I can even see their faces, so it's much better than a phone call.

Speaker 3 Well, um, I'm a webmaster, so the Internet is very important for my job. I work with different websites, first of all creating them and then making sure that everyone can use them. I also try to make existing websites work faster. I enjoy my job because I love computers and solving problems.

Speaker 4 Yeah, I spend a lot of time on the Internet every day. It's a great way to keep in touch with friends and also to meet new people. There's one site I use a lot to talk to my friends, upload photos, and post videos that I find funny. I also like looking at my friends' profiles to see what they're doing.

12 A))

H = Host, **C** = Christopher
H Hello, and welcome to *Movie Madness*. In the studio with us today is movie critic Christopher Phillips. We've asked him to choose his two favorite movie adaptations of books. Christopher, where are you going to start?
C Well, it's been a difficult choice but I'm going to start with a very early movie, the 1946 adaptation of *Great Expectations* by Charles Dickens.
H 1946? That is early.
C Yes, and as you can imagine, the movie is in black and white. It tells the story of a poor young boy named Pip who with the help of a mysterious person, becomes a gentleman. The story doesn't change much in the movie, but the photography makes the atmosphere darker and more frightening. It's an excellent adaptation.
H *Great Expectations*. OK. I haven't seen the movie, but I've read the book, of course. What's your other movie, Christopher?
C Well, my other choice is more recent. It's *The English Patient*.
H Yes, I've seen that one a few times. But I don't know anything about the book. Tell us more.
C Well, the author is a Sri Lankan-Canadian writer named Michael Ondaatje, and his novel won an important prize – the Booker Prize. The movie came out in 1996, and it's a wonderful adaptation of the book. It tells the story of a man in a military hospital who has been in a plane crash. We also learn something about the life and loves of his nurse. Again, there are a few changes to the story, but the best thing about the movie is the choice of actors, who are perfect for their parts. The movie won a total of nine Oscars, which shows just how good it is.
H Christopher Phillips, thank you for joining us.
C Thank you for having me. I've enjoyed it.

12 B))

Speaker 1 **I** = Interviewer, **S** = Speaker 1
I Have you ever been to Africa?

S Yes, I have. I've been to Kenya.
I When did you go?
S I went in 2010. We stayed with some friends who are living in Nairobi. While we were there, we went on a trip to Tsavo East, which is an enormous national park. Unfortunately, our car broke down in the park, and the guards took six hours to rescue us. It was really scary!

Speaker 2 **I** = Interviewer, **S** = Speaker 2
I Have you ever been to South America?
S Yes, I have. I've been to Brazil.
I When did you go?
S I went there in 2006 on a business trip. In fact, we were at a conference, so it wasn't very hard work. We stayed in a five-star hotel, and the company paid for everything.

Speaker 3 **I** = Interviewer, **S** = Speaker 3
I Have you ever been to Australia?
S Well, I haven't been to Australia, but I've been to New Zealand.
I When did you go?
S I went with my wife when we got married in 2011. We stayed in a luxury apartment on the banks of Lake Wakatipu, and we had a great time doing a lot of different water sports. The best moment for me, though, was when we did a bungee jump from the Kawarau Bridge. It was really exciting!

Speaker 4 **I** = Interviewer, **S** = Speaker 4
I Have you ever been to Asia?
S Yes, I have. I've been to Thailand.
I When did you go?
S I went with my family in 2006. We stayed in a special hotel in the jungle, and we slept in a treehouse. But the most amazing part of our trip happened when we visited Bangkok. We were lucky enough to be there for Songkran, the Thai New Year, so we saw the water festival. You know, the one where everybody throws water at each other in the street!

12 C))

New Zealand. Home of Middle Earth. And the best way to experience it is on our *Lord of the Rings* Edoras tour. The tour leaves Christchurch at 9 a.m. and returns at 6 p.m., but we can pick you up at other central city locations, too. The groups are small, and the guides are friendly and informative. You don't need to be a *Lord of the Rings* fan to enjoy the tour because the scenery is fantastic. Transportation is in a Land Rover, and we take you through the spectacular mountains of the Southern Alps where you can see clear lakes and blue rivers, and you can breathe fresh mountain air. Our destination is Mount Sunday, the real-life mountain that in the movie is Edoras, the capital city of the Rohan people. While you're there, you can use some the most famous items from the movie: Aragorn's sword, Gimli's axe, and the flag of Rohan. For lunch, there is a luxury picnic, which we eat outside in the open air. Visit our store at the end of your trip and buy exclusive Lord of the Rings souvenirs for your family and friends back home.

The tour runs daily throughout the year, and you can buy tickets online. The price includes your pick up and drop off, your trip in the Land Rover, your guided walk to the very top of Edoras, and your delicious lunch. Tickets cost $135 for adults, per person, and $94 for children aged 14 and under.

So, what are you waiting for? Book your tickets now before you miss your chance to see one of the most beautiful *Lord of the Rings* locations. It's an experience you'll never forget.

OXFORD
UNIVERSITY PRESS

198 Madison Avenue
New York, NY 10016 USA

Great Clarendon Street, Oxford, ox2 6dp, United Kingdom

Oxford University Press is a department of the University of Oxford.
It furthers the University's objective of excellence in research, scholarship,
and education by publishing worldwide. Oxford is a registered trade
mark of Oxford University Press in the UK and in certain other countries

General Manager: Laura Pearson
Executive Publishing Manager: Erik Gundersen
Senior Managing Editor: Louisa VanHouten
Associate Editor: Hana Yoo
Design Director: Susan Sanguily
Associate Design Manager: Michael Steinhofer
Image Manager: Trisha Masterson
Image Editor: Liaht Pashayan
Electronic Production Manager: Julie Armstrong
Production Coordinator: Brad Tucker

ISBN: 978 0 19 477639 4 Workbook (pack)
ISBN: 978 0 19 477603 5 Workbook (pack component)
ISBN: 978 0 19 477670 7 IChecker (pack component)

Printed in China

This book is printed on paper from certified and well-managed sources

ACKNOWLEDGEMENTS

*The authors and publisher are grateful to those who have given permission to reproduce the
following extracts and adaptations of copyright material:*

p.38 Extract from Oxford Bookworms Library Starter: *Sally's Phone* by Christine
Lindop © Oxford University Press 2007. Reproduced by Permission; p.81 Extract
from "Lord of the Rings – New Zealand," from http://www.tourism.net.nz.
Reproduced by permission of New Zealand Tourism Guide.

Sources: p.77 http://blog.moviefone.com; p.81 http://www.hasslefree.co.nz

*We would also like to thank the following for permission to reproduce the following
photographs:*

Illustrations by: Cover: Chellie Carroll; Barb Bastian pp.25; Peter Bull pp. 10, 49;
Clive Goodyear pp.8, 15, 20, 50, 52, 69; Atushi Hara /Dutch Uncle Agency pp.4, 5,
58, 67; Sophie Joyce pp.11, 12; Tim Marrs pp.61; Jerome Mireault/Colagene p.13;
Roger Penwill pp.30, 33, 54.

*We would also like to thank the following for permission to reproduce the following
photographs:*

Cover: Gemenacom/shutterstock.com; Andrey_Popov/shutterstock.com;
Wavebreakmedia/shutterstock.com; Image Source/Getty Images; Lane Oatey/
Blue Jean Images/Getty Images; BJI/Blue Jean Images/Getty Images; Image Source/
Corbis; Yuri Arcurs/Tetra Images/Corbis; Wavebreak Media Ltd./Corbis; pg. 7
(Yin) zhang bo/Getty Images, (Carlos) OUP/Cultura, (Moira) OUP/Image Source;
pg. 10 (Harbor) Richard Cummins/Corbis, (Marlowe) Courtesy of Hotel Marlowe,
(Sheraton) Starwood Hotels & Resorts Worldwide, Inc.; pg. 11 (coin) Chimpinski/
Shutterstock.com, (family) Creatas/Jupiterimages, (newspaper) Martin Shields/
Alamy, (ticket) Marco Simola/Photographers Direct, (wallet) LA Heukisinkveld/
Alamy, (all others) MM Studios; pg. 18 (flag) OUP/Graphi-Ogre, (subway) Tim
Clayton/Corbis, (Lina) Cultura/Kris Ubach and Quim Roser/Getty Images,
(Julianna) Jacqueline Veissid/Getty Images, (Hannah) OUP/Image Source; pg. 19
(1) Image100/ Photolibrary Group, (2) Andrew Brookes/Corbis UK Ltd., (3) Monty
Rakusen/cultura/Corbis UK Ltd., (4) Tetra Images/Photolibrary Group, (5) OUP/
Tetra Images, (6) OUP/Corbis, (7) Custom Medical Stock Photo/Alamy, (8) David
Young-Wolff/ Alamy, (9) Garry Wade/ Getty Images, (10) Tetra Images/Alamy; pg.
22 (dinner) christophe viseux/Alamy, (facebook logo) digitallife/Alamy, (texting)
JGI/Jamie Grill/Blend Images/Corbis; pg. 24 (grandmother) Tony Metaxas/Getty
Images, (grandfather) RedChopsticks/Getty Images; pg. 26 (Tyler) Yuri Arcurs/
Alamy, (Elena) JGI/Getty Images, (Yejoon) Multi-bits/Getty Images; pg. 27 Ocean/
Corbis; pg. 28 (Becky) Corbis RF/Alamy, (Matt) Tetra Images/Corbis; pg. 29 Tom
Stewart/Corbis; pg. 31 (1,4) Photolibrary/Fancy/Getty Images, (2) Ghislain & Marie
David de Lossy/Getty Images, (3) OUP/Image Source, (5) Fran and Helena/Culture/
Corbis, (6) DON EMMERT/AFP/Getty Images, (7) Photolibrary/Fancy/Getty Images,
(8) Mark Romanelli/Getty Images, (9) Digital Vision/Getty Images, (10) Image
Source/Alamy, (11) Corbis, (12a) Jim Naughten/Corbis, (12d) Photolibrary/Getty
Images, (13) Shepic/Alamy, (14) Oliver Rossi/Getty Images; pg. 32 John Giustina/
Getty Images; pg. 34 (1) Pete Turner/Getty Images, (2) Carl & Ann Purcell/Corbis, (3)
Stefan Sollfors/Alamy, (4) Jose Luis Pelaez, Inc./Corbis, (5) Image Source/Corbis, (6)
Mike Theiss/National Geographic Society/Corbis, (7) Vincent Lowe/Alamy, (8) Paul
Burns/Corbis; pg. 35 (Red Rocks) Blaine Harrington III/Alamy, (Denver) AP Photo/
Ed Andrieski, (Glennwood) Walter Bibikow/Getty Images; pg. 36 John Connell/
Getty Images; pg. 37 James Whitaker/Getty Images; pg. 39 (William) Camarena/
Image Source, (Amanda) OUP/Image Source; pg. 41 (Rihanna) Picture Perfect/Rex
Features, (Bach) Lebrecht Music and Arts Photo Library/Alamy, (Beethoven) GL
Archive/Alamy, (Black Eyed Peas) Rex Features, (concert) NBCU Photobank/Rex
Features, (Cullum) Isopix/Rex Features, (Iron Maiden) Steve Thorne/Redferns/Getty
Images, (J-Lo) BDG/Rex Features, (Joe Lee Hooker) Rex Features, (Reggae) Bash/Sipa
Press/Rex Features; pg. 44 (Reagan) Alliance Images/Alamy, (Lincoln, Washington)
Corbis, (King) Bettmann/Corbis, (Franklin) Time & Life Pictures/Getty Images,
(Copeland) Aaron Copland Collection; Music Division, Library of Congress; pg. 46
Julian Finney/Getty Images; pg. 47 Wavebreak Media Ltd./Corbis; pg. 48 Beau Lark/
Corbis; pg. 49 (car) Mike Dobel/Alamy, (bus) Per Makitalo/Getty Images, (train)
Transtock/Masterfile; pg. 51 Radius Images/Alamy; pg. 54 Paulo Whitaker /Reuters/
Corbis; pg. 55 Maesmawr Hall Hotel/Karen Blakeman; pg. 56 MM Studios; pg. 57
(camel) OUP/Photodisc, (coconut) Richard Watson/Getty Images, (icicle) Lucie Lang/
Alamy; pg. 59 Maximilian Stock Ltd./Getty Images; pg. 64 (1) Paul Doyle/Alamy,
(2) OUP/Bananastock, (3) John Guillemin/Bloomberg/ Getty Images, (4) Kiursty
McLaren/Alamy, (5) Motoring Picture Library/Alamy, (6) David L. Moore/ Alamy,
(7) Peter Crome/Alamy, (8) incamerastock/Alamy, (9) Homer Sykes/Alamy, (10) Les
Ladbury/Alamy, (11) BL Images /Alamy; pg. 65 Jutta Klee/ableimages/Corbis; pg.
68 Anna Idestam-Almquist/Alamy; pg. 70 (Iceland) Jon Arnold Images Ltd/Alamy,
(Canada) Scott Tysick/Masterfile; pg. 72 (1) iofoto/shutterstock.com, (2) Jose Luis
Pelaez, Inc./Blend Images/Corbis, (3) Image Source; pg. 73 Axaulya/istockphoto.
com; pg. 74 Photo Provider Network/Alamy; pg. 77 Mark Johnson Productions/The
Kobal Collection; pg. 79 Ethan Miller/Getty Images; pg. 81 (New Zealand) Stuart
Barry/Alamy, (LOTR) New Line/Saul Zaentz/Wig Nut/The Kobal Collection